Speaking, Listening & Understanding

Games for Young Children

Catherine Delamain & Jill Spring

Speechmark Publishing

Telford Road, Bicester, Oxon OX26 4LQ, UK

Please note that in this text, for reasons of clarity alone,
'he' is used to refer to the child and 'she' to the teacher.

First published in 2003 by
Speechmark Publishing Ltd, Telford Road, Bicester, Oxon OX26 4LQ, UK

www.speechmark.net

© Catherine Delamain & Jill Spring, 2003
 Reprinted 2004

This edition produced for Bookspan,1271 Avenue of the Americas, New York, NY 10020, USA

002-5139/Printed in the United Kingdom/1010

A CIP catalogue record for this book is available from the British Library.

ISBN 0 86388 561 6

Contents

Preface

'The limits of my language mean the limits of my world'
(L Wittgenstein, *Tractatus Logico-Philosophicus*)

This book contains a collection of games and activities designed to foster the speaking, listening and understanding skills of children in mainstream schools. The games are aimed at children in Key Stage 1 of the National Curriculum of England and Wales, in Years 1 and 2. These children will range in age from five to seven years. The English syllabus acknowledges the vital role of speaking, listening and understanding. This book aims to identify some of the ways in which language can be used, and provide activities to help children become effective communicators. The authors are both experienced speech and language therapists who have worked extensively alongside mainstream teachers for many years, and have seen the benefits of collaborative practice. They are aware of the enormous pressure teachers work under, and have tried to make the activities both teacher- and child-friendly by minimising paperwork and linking with the existing National Curriculum. They offer this collection of games as a practical tool for developing functional language.

Speaking, Listening and Understanding: Games for Young Children offers:

◆ A wide range of carefully structured activities

◆ Clear aims and instructions

◆ An extensive resource section

◆ Opportunities for assessment, target-setting, and evaluation.

Acknowledgements

The authors would like to thank the staff in all the schools in which they have tried out some of these activities. Particular thanks go to Gillingham Primary School, Damer's First School and Winterbourne Valley First School, in Dorset.

Introduction

'It is the possibility of making sense that stimulates children to learn'
(David Booth, *Guiding the Reading Process*)

Language is fundamental to learning. It is the main medium for teaching. Children need to be able to listen to what they are told, and then to understand it, think about it and remember it. They also need to be able to use language themselves to ask questions, seek clarification, negotiate, compromise and solve problems.

Language is also vital for the development of emotional literacy and the acquisition of social skills. It is the framework on which the control of behaviour is built, at first by adults, but increasingly by the child through self-directed internal language. Much of this learning takes place in the context of the family before the child ever reaches school, but it is an ongoing process throughout the school years. Children who cannot communicate effectively through spoken language will struggle to cope with the negotiations, explanations, and compromise essential for satisfactory social relationships. Faced with a playground dispute and no way of 'talking it through', how will they react? Unfortunately, their only means of expression may be aggression.

In our increasingly technological world, where most children spend much of their leisure time watching television or playing computer games, opportunities for developing communication skills are diminishing, and we therefore have a responsibility to try to redress the balance in school.

The National Curriculum pays much attention to language enrichment and the development of general and topic-related vocabulary. However, while desirable targets for speaking and listening are cited, these are very broad, loosely defined, and consequently difficult to measure. While there is growing awareness that children need to develop communication skills, opportunities to practise specific aspects of language are not addressed in the curriculum, and appropriate resources available to teachers are limited.

The ability to listen and understand, and to communicate effectively using spoken language, are essential precursors to using written language, yet we do little in a structured way to help children develop these skills.

These games are designed for whole-class use, but it is recognised that between 5 and 7 per cent of children in Years 1 and 2, aged five and six years old, will have identifiable language difficulties. These children are clearly at a disadvantage, and learn to cope in a variety of ways. Some try to fade into the background; some react to frustration by lashing out physically; some try to compensate by becoming the classroom clown, and some just give up. The activities will help reinforce existing language therapy programmes. There will be a number of other children whose language skills are poorly developed, and who will also benefit from this structured approach.

How to use this Book

Speaking, Listening and Understanding: Games for Young Children is divided into three main sections: 'Understanding Spoken Language'; 'Using Spoken Language', and 'Teaching Resources'. The two main sections are subdivided into five different skill areas. There are 16 activities in each skill area, in four ability stages – Stage I being the easiest, and Stage IV the hardest.

We have designed the activities to fit into the existing curriculum as far as possible. The tabs down the side of each page suggest which area of the curriculum best suits that particular activity, and also indicate the ability stage.

Each activity includes a clear aim; the equipment and preparation required; clear instructions and, where appropriate, additional tips and ways of extending the activity. There is an extensive Teaching Resources section containing texts and pictures to be used with specific activities. Equipment and preparation has been kept to a minimum, but where it is necessary this is clearly indicated.

Although the authors have made reference to the National Curriculum of England and Wales, the activities are not dependent on knowledge or experience of the National Curriculum, and can be carried out by any English-speaking user. (See 'Notes for Users Outside the UK' below.)

THE SKILL AREAS

Understanding Spoken Language

▲ *Following Instructions*
Activities to promote careful, active listening to unambiguous spoken instructions of increasing length and complexity.

▲ *Getting the Main Idea*
Activities to help children grasp the key information in games, stories and non-fiction text.

▲ *Thinking Skills*
Activities to encourage children to develop 'internal conversations' to help them to solve problems.

▲ *Developing Vocabulary*
Activities to practise the use of essential vocabulary, with particular emphasis on vocabulary used in numeracy.

▲ *Drawing Inference*
Activities to promote an awareness of underlying meanings and implications.

Using Spoken Language

▲ *Narrating*
Activities that give children opportunities to develop story-telling and reporting skills.

▲ *Describing*
Activities to encourage the use of descriptive language, and extend the vocabulary of adjectives.

▲ *Explaining*
Activities to develop children's ability to give clear explanations, and to be aware when the explanation needs further clarification.

▲ *Predicting*
Activities to practise making verbal predictions based on pre-existing knowledge or given information.

▲ *Playing with Words*
Activities to develop awareness of rhyme, syllable knowledge and alliteration, and encourage enjoyment of onomatopoeia, verbal jokes and double meanings.

ESTABLISHING STARTING LEVELS

The games are grouped in Stages I–IV, from easy to harder. The Stages do not correspond rigidly to age, but progress broadly along developmental lines. Stage I is likely to be the preferred starting point for children at the beginning of Year 1 (age 5–6 years). As with any activity, there will be considerable variation in the children's abilities, and different groups of children can be moved on through the stages at their own speed. More linguistically able children are likely to have completed Stage IV before the end of Year 2 (age 6–7 years).

TARGET-SETTING

You may have children in your class who have Individual Education Plans. Many of the activities could be used as part of the Individual Education Plan (IEP) target-setting process, as have activities from the authors' previous book, *Developing Baseline Communication Skills*. Each activity has a particular aim, which is worded in accordance with target-setting protocol.

RECORD-KEEPING

There are optional record-keeping forms to enable you to monitor progress. These are divided into Understanding Spoken Language and Using Spoken Language. The names of the children are entered in the left-hand column. A key suggesting how progress is recorded appears at the top of each form. Using the forms in this way will indicate individual children's strengths and weaknesses, and so aid in future planning.

NOTES FOR USERS OUTSIDE THE UK

◆ The National Curriculum of England and Wales provides a statutory entitlement to learning for all pupils. It provides a syllabus for all subjects, with clearly stated attainment targets and a structure for monitoring progress.

◆ 'Circle Time' refers to whole-group teaching sessions where the teacher leads a variety of activities to promote listening skills, group interaction and social communication skills.

◆ The 'Literacy Hour' is a structured approach to teaching basic literacy skills to children between the ages of five and 11 years. It is divided into word, sentence and text levels, thereby addressing phonics, grammar, and creative writing skills.

◆ The 'Numeracy Hour' is a structured approach to teaching mathematics and number skills.

◆ In the Teaching Resources, UK currency occurs within some activities. If necessary, alter the currency to match that of the user's country. The same applies to mention of specific sports teams.

FOLLOWING INSTRUCTIONS

Stage I

Stage II

Stage III

Stage IV

Circle Time

Hall/PE

Literacy

Numeracy

Drama

Small Group

Art

Humanities

Science

FOLLOWING INSTRUCTIONS

Making Statues

Aim
To be able to follow two-stage instructions containing four ideas.

Equipment

None.

How to Play

Tell the children to spread out around the room. Explain that they are going to turn into statues. You will tell them how to stand or sit, and they must then keep very still while you come around to check if they are doing the right thing. People who have not followed the instructions correctly are eliminated. The last child in is the winner.

Examples

Put one hand in the air and shut your eyes.
Open your eyes and put your hand down.
Put both arms up in the air and stand on one leg.
Put your arms down and sit on the floor.
Put one finger on your nose and shut your eyes.
Open your eyes and put both hands on your head.
Take your hands off your head and lie down on the floor.
Roll over on your tummy and close your eyes.

Tip

The instructions need to follow each other, as in the example above.

Extension

Vary the instructions by occasionally saying 'Don't … (put your arms down, open your eyes, take your hands off your head).' This will eliminate quite a number of children! Then carry on as before.

Speechmark

FOLLOWING INSTRUCTIONS

Stage I

Stage II

Stage III

Stage IV

Circle Time

Hall/PE

Literacy

Numeracy

Drama

Small Group

Art

Humanities

Science

Hoops and Bean-bags

Aim

To be able to carry out instructions involving movement and position.

A bean-bag and a hoop for each child.

You need a large space to play this game – for example, the hall. Arrange the hoops and bean-bags in a line, about a metre away from a wall, well spaced apart. Tell the children they are going to have a race game, but they must listen carefully and move in the right kind of way. If necessary do a demonstration. Call out an instruction, and when you say 'Go!', everyone must go to the right object, moving in the right way. Anyone who ends up by the wrong object, or moves in the wrong way, is out.

Run to a bean-bag. Crawl to a hoop. Jump in a hoop. Walk sideways to a bean-bag. Hop to a hoop. Stand beside a bean-bag. Sit in front of a hoop.

You can make this more competitive by removing a bean-bag and a hoop after each instruction, so that one person will be out each time.

Stage I

Stage II

Stage III

Stage IV

Circle Time

Hall/PE

Literacy

Numeracy

Drama

Small Group

Art

Humanities

Science

FOLLOWING INSTRUCTIONS

Musical Bean-bags

Aim
To be able to remember and carry out an instruction accurately.

A bean-bag for each member of the group.
Music.

This game is essentially the same as Musical Chairs. However, in this variation the children must move to the bean-bags in the way you tell them. Anyone not moving in the right way is out. Scatter the bean-bags on the floor around the room, well spaced. Give the instruction before you switch on the music. When you put the music on, everyone has to walk slowly around the room. When the music stops, each child should move to a bean-bag in the way you told them.

When the music stops, crawl to a bean-bag.
When the music stops, jump to a bean-bag.
When the music stops, skip to a bean-bag.
When the music stops, walk very slowly to a bean-bag.

If possible have another adult help to monitor the activity.

FOLLOWING INSTRUCTIONS

Stage I

Stage II

Stage III

Stage IV

Circle Time

Hall/PE

Literacy

Numeracy

Drama

Small Group

Art

Humanities

Science

Jewellery Shop

Aim

To be able to carry out two-stage instructions involving number and colour.

Equipment

'Jewellery Shop' template from Teaching Resources coloured in different patterns.
Enough coloured beads for each child, and a threading lace each.

How to Play

Tell the children they are going to make some necklaces to go in the 'jeweller's shop'. You will call out which beads they are to use. Choose one of the bead pictures from the template, but do not let the children see it. Call out instructions that match your bead picture – for example, 'Two red beads and then one yellow one.' (Pause until everyone has finished.) 'Three blue beads and then two green ones.' (Pause again, and so on until the necklaces are completed.) Hold up your picture for the children to see, and let them compare their necklaces with it.

Tip

It may be useful to give the instructions again slowly as the children compare their necklace with the picture. Make the game more interesting by inventing customers for each necklace the children make – for example, a princess, a film star, a character from a story or a TV programme.

Stage I

Stage II

Stage III

Stage IV

Circle Time

Hall/PE

Literacy

Numeracy

Drama

Small Group

Art

Humanities

Science

FOLLOWING INSTRUCTIONS

Curtain Up!

Aim
To be able to carry out a realistic mime based on received information.

Teacher will need to prepare scenarios with a role for each member of the group.

Tell the group that they are going to pretend to be characters in a play. Explain that you are going to read the instructions at the beginning of the play, and you want them to pretend to be doing the actions. Remind them that they will need to listen carefully for their names and remember the activity. Then read the short scenario. When you have read it, tell the children to get into position, doing their action. The length of this activity depends on the group. You may be able to repeat it two or three times within the session.

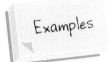

Scenario: It was Saturday afternoon. Amy was digging the garden; Ben was planting seeds; Kylie was trying to catch the pet rabbit; Abdul was hanging out the washing, and Rashid was watching football on TV.

FOLLOWING INSTRUCTIONS

Stage I

Stage II

Stage III

Stage IV

Circle Time

Hall/PE

Literacy

Numeracy

Drama

Small Group

Art

Humanities

Science

Find It

Aim
To be able to find an item by its description.

Equipment

Classroom items, see examples.

Preparation

Write descriptions of everyday items found in the classroom. Do not give too much information about each item – see examples below.

How to Play

Divide the group into two teams, A and B. Explain that you will be giving a description of something in the classroom to both teams. They must listen carefully, and when you say 'Go!', the first member of each team must find something that matches that description. The first to find a suitable item wins a point for their team. Continue until all the children have had a go. The winning team is the one with the most points.

Examples

Ruler – a long, narrow plastic object.
Jug – a container with a handle that is good for pouring.
Paperclip – a useful metal object for fastening things together.
Paintbrush – a long thin object with bristles.
Key – a metal object that opens things.

Tip

You will need to adjust the descriptions to match the age and ability of the children.

Stage I

Stage II

Stage III

Stage IV

Circle Time

Hall/PE

Literacy

Numeracy

Drama

Small Group

Art

Humanities

Science

FOLLOWING INSTRUCTIONS

Witch's Brew

Aim
To be able to retain and carry out simple spoken instructions.

Equipment

Paint, mixing palettes, paintbrushes and paper.

How to Play

This is a game for up to six players. Tell the children they are going to help Wanda the Witch make a spell. To do this they will need to listen carefully to the paint-mixing instructions. Each item that goes in the cauldron has to be a different colour. This spell needs six things if the magic is to work: a lizard, a snake, a snail shell, a dragon's tooth, a bat wing, and a rotten apple. Assign one item to each child, and write it in pencil on their sheet of paper. Then tell them which colours they will need to mix. They must wait until all the instructions have been given. The child with the best memory and powers of concentration should be the first to get their instruction. Once all the instructions have been given, the children can start mixing their paint. They can then paint the item using their paint. When everyone has finished painting, check that all the items are the right colour.

Examples

lizard	= blue + yellow	(green)
snake	= red + yellow	(orange)
snail shell	= red + green	(shade of brown)
dragon's tooth	= blue + red	(purple)
bat wing	= black + blue	(very dark blue)
rotten apple	= red + black	(dark brown/grey shade)

Speechmark

FOLLOWING INSTRUCTIONS

Stage I

Stage II

Stage III

Stage IV

Circle Time

Hall/PE

Literacy

Numeracy

Drama

Small Group

Art

Humanities

Science

Magic Cauldron

Aim
To be able to follow instructions involving colour and number, and to make decisions about who shall move.

Equipment

Team colours.

How to Play

Put the children into team colours so that they know whether they are yellows, blues, greens, reds, and so on. Tell the children to spread out around the room. Mark out an area of the room, by drawing a chalk circle, laying skipping ropes in a circle, or using chairs or benches to indicate a space. This area is the Magic Cauldron. Tell the children you are a witch or wizard, and you are going to mix spells using lots of different colours. When the mixture is just right, a magic creature will be produced.

You will call out instructions: 'three yellows into the cauldron'; 'two blues into the cauldron'; 'one yellow come out'; 'four reds in'; 'one blue out', and so on. When you decide the moment is right, announce that the spell is finished and the witch has made their magic creature.

Tips

This game involves the children in making decisions among themselves as to who shall go into or out of the cauldron, since sometimes you will say, for example, 'two reds come out', and there may be three reds in the cauldron at that moment. They will probably need guidance at first as to how to reach the decisions, but the game gives useful practice in thinking skills.

It will make things more interesting if you can have three or four toy creatures hidden in a bag, and produce one as each spell is completed.

Stage I

Stage II

Stage III

Stage IV

Circle Time

Hall/PE

Literacy

Numeracy

Drama

Small Group

Art

Humanities

Science

FOLLOWING INSTRUCTIONS

Puppet Show

Aim
To be able to listen to a short instruction and collect up to three items.

Equipment

A simple glove puppet.
A list of scenarios (see examples).
Suitable items to match the scenarios.

How to Play

Introduce Ping the Puppet. Tell the children that Ping is very disorganised and never has the things he needs. Choose a fairly confident child to start the activity. Explain the first scenario – for example, 'Ping is going to do a painting. He needs a piece of paper, a paintbrush and some paints'. Then ask the child to collect the items. Let the rest of the group check whether they are right or not. Continue until every child in the group has had a turn collecting. To finish, let Ping ask each child why he needed those particular items.

Examples

The following scenarios are suggestions for what Ping is up to. Feel free to make up your own!
Paint a picture.
Wrap up a present.
Make a birthday card.
Play 'Snakes and Ladders'.
Clean out the classroom pet.

FOLLOWING INSTRUCTIONS

Stage I

Stage II

Stage III

Stage IV

Circle Time

Hall/PE

Literacy

Numeracy

Drama

Small Group

Art

Humanities

Science

Round Up

Aim
To be able to follow instructions containing three ideas (animal/colour/length).

Equipment

Paper tails, some long and some short, of varying colours.

Preparation

Draw, cut out and colour the tails, enough for all the children.

How to Play

Attach a tail to each child, tucked into the back of trousers or the top of skirts.
Divide the children into two groups, standing well apart. Explain that one group is composed of mice and the other group is composed of squirrels. Choose one child as a catcher and tell the child, for example, 'Go and bring me a mouse with a long green tail' or 'Go and bring me a squirrel with a short red tail.' When the child has found a mouse or squirrel with a tail that answers the description, they go and join that group, while the child who has been found becomes the catcher.

Extension

Increase the number of different animal groups.

FOLLOWING INSTRUCTIONS

Dotty

Aim
To be able to follow spoken instructions relating to written numbers.

Dot-to-dot sheets (photocopiable sheets available in Teaching Resources) and pencils.

Copy enough dot-to-dot sheets for each child to have one.

Tell the children to place their pencil on START. Tell them you will call out a number, and they should draw a line from the START to that number. Then they will be given the next number to go to, and so on. Explain that the numbers are all jumbled up, not in order like the usual dot-to-dot picture, so they will have to listen carefully or their picture will not look right. At the end of the game they should all have the same recognisable picture.

Number patterns:

Flower and Bee: 1 (Start), 3, 7, 5, 4, 2, 10, 8, 9, 6, 11, 14, 20, 12, 23, 15, 22, 16, 21, 18, 13, 24, 19, 17, 25, 26 (Finish)

Train: 1 (Start), 8, 3, 6, 10, 5, 2, 14, 7, 4, 9, 15, 11, 20, 12, 17, 13, 19, 16, 21, 18, 23, 22, 24 (Finish)

Sidebar navigation
Stage I

Stage II

Stage III

Stage IV

Circle Time

Hall/PE

Literacy

Numeracy

Drama

Small Group

Art

Humanities

Science

Labels
Equipment

Preparation

How to Play

FOLLOWING INSTRUCTIONS

Stage I

Stage II

Stage III

Stage IV

Circle Time

Hall/PE

Literacy

Numeracy

Drama

Small Group

Art

Humanities

Science

Chicken Food

Aim
To be able to follow instructions containing four ideas.

Equipment

Draw a selection of pictures as listed in the examples below.

Preparation

Photocopy and cut out the pictures.

How to Play

Seat the children in small groups (not more than three or four) around their tables. Spread out a selection of the pictures on each table. Tell the children that you will be describing one picture at a time. When they think they know which picture they are looking for, they can sort through the pile using just the first and second fingers of one hand, like a chicken's beak. If they find the picture they are looking for, they can pull it towards themselves with their two fingers. Once it gets to their edge of the table they can claim it. From time to time, two children will find the same picture and pull at it from opposite directions. This is good practice for losing gracefully! If a picture tears, the child with the larger piece claims it.

Examples

A big black hat on a bed.
A small black hat on a bed.
A big black hat on a chair.
A small black hat on a table.
A big white box on a bed.
A small white box on a chair.

FOLLOWING INSTRUCTIONS

Stage I

Stage II

Stage III

Stage IV

Circle Time

Hall/PE

Literacy

Numeracy

Drama

Small Group

Art

Humanities

Science

Holiday Snaps

Aim

To be able to follow instructions to complete a picture.

'Holiday Snaps' templates from Teaching Resources.
'Holiday Snaps' texts from Teaching Resources.

Choose either the beach or the country scene, and make a copy for each child. Give out pencils and colouring material. Tell the children you are going to give them some instructions to finish the picture. Read each instruction twice, and allow time for them to draw and colour as required. At the end, everyone can mark the items they put in their picture. The winner is the person who got the highest number of points.

The sun was shining. There were three little clouds in the sky. Far out at sea was a little red fishing boat with a blue sail.

This could form the basis of a piece of writing – for example, a postcard, in the Literacy Hour.

FOLLOWING INSTRUCTIONS

Stage I

Stage II

Stage III

Stage IV

Circle Time

Hall/PE

Literacy

Numeracy

Drama

Small Group

Art

Humanities

Science

Talkative Teacher

Aim

To be able to sort out the important points from a lot of irrelevant verbiage.

Equipment

A pencil and paper for each child.

How to Play

Explain to the children that today teacher has swallowed some 'talking medicine' by mistake, and just cannot stop talking. Among all the chatter, the teacher will be telling them things she really wants them to do. The children are to listen carefully, and when they spot an instruction, they are to carry it out. When the teacher stops talking, she will look at their papers and see how many people spotted all the instructions. An example is given below, but after a bit of practice it is quite easy to make it up as you go along, including different instructions each time.

Examples

'Now children, I want you to be very clever and listen very carefully, and I'd like you to *draw a circle on your paper*, like good children, and you all know how to do that, and then I want you to *put a little dot in the middle of the circle*, just a little one, and after that I want you please to try very hard and *put a cross outside the circle*, anywhere you like, you are doing so well, and then the last thing I would like you to do is to *draw a little star at the bottom of the page*, do you think you have managed all of that?' (Four items.)

Tips

Try to sit the children apart from each other, to discourage copying.
After a practice run or two, speed up your delivery.

Stage I

Stage II

Stage III

Stage IV

Circle Time

Hall/PE

Literacy

Numeracy

Drama

Small Group

Art

Humanities

Science

FOLLOWING INSTRUCTIONS

Amazing Mazes

Aim
To be able to follow instructions, including left and right, to reach the centre of a maze.

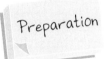

Maze pictures from Teaching Resources.

Make photocopies of one of the mazes, enough for each child to have one.

Give each child a copy of the maze. Read out the accompanying instructions, slowly enough for the children to mark each move with their pencils.
Treasure Chest: Start at the botom. Up – right – up to the corner – left – down – left – down – right – down – left.
Sheep: Start at the bottom. Up – left – up – right – up – right – up – right – down – left – up.

Remember that if you are showing them 'left' and 'right', as may be necessary more than once, when you are facing the children your left will be *their* right!

FOLLOWING INSTRUCTIONS

Letter Strings

Aim

To be able to carry out instructions involving letters of the alphabet.

Equipment

A sheet of paper each and a pencil.

Preparation

The sheets of paper should be ruled into a grid containing approximately eight columns and six rows. Prepare your own sheet, by writing letters in each box on the grid. In the example below, these form a phrase when read backwards.

How to Play

Tell the children you have a secret code in your hand. You are going to read out the letters and they must write each one in a separate box, working from left to right. Demonstrate what you mean. For the first attempt, read each letter singly. At the end of the row, hold up your letter string, and see how many children can match it. See if anyone can work out the code – you will need to tell them that it is written backwards. When they are confident about listening to single letters, make it more difficult by saying two letters at a time.

Examples

s	t	a	c	e	k	i	l	i

| Stage I |
| Stage II |
| Stage III |
| **Stage IV** |
| Circle Time |
| Hall/PE |
| **Literacy** |
| Numeracy |
| Drama |
| **Small Group** |
| Art |
| Humanities |
| Science |

Speaking, Listening & Understanding
UNDERSTANDING SPOKEN LANGUAGE

DEVELOPING VOCABULARY

Stage I

Stage II

Stage III

Stage IV

Circle Time

Hall/PE

Literacy

Numeracy

Drama

Small Group

Art

Humanities

Science

DEVELOPING VOCABULARY

Bizzo's World

Aim

To understand the vocabulary: 'next to', 'edge of', 'side', 'top', 'bottom', 'in front of', 'behind'.

A copy of 'Bizzo's World' template for each child.
Suitable drawing and colouring equipment.

Tell the children that you would like them to draw some of the objects and creatures that Bizzo can see when he's out and about. Give each instruction twice. The first time the children listen carefully. After you have repeated the instruction, they draw the item where they think it should be.

Draw a duck *next to* the pond.
Draw a tree at the *edge of* the field.
Draw a tractor at the *bottom* of the hill.
Draw a rabbit *beside* one of the trees.
There are some flowers growing on *top* of the hill.
Put a bicycle *in front of* Bizzo's cottage.
Colour in the tree *next to* the pond.
You can just about see a football *behind* the gate at the *top* of the field.

Speechmark

DEVELOPING VOCABULARY

Stage I

Stage II

Stage III

Stage IV

Circle Time

Hall/PE

Literacy

Numeracy

Drama

Small Group

Art

Humanities

Science

Snakes and Ladders

Aim
To play a game that involves understanding the words 'forwards' and 'backwards' .

Equipment

A bag of instruction slips (available for cutting up in Teaching Resources).
Two bean-bags.

How to Play

Chalk two twenty-rung ladders on the floor, with gaps between the rungs large enough for a child to stand in. Divide the children into two teams, one at the bottom of each ladder.
The first child from each team comes to the teacher and draws an instruction slip out of the bag. They can read the instruction themselves if they are able, otherwise the teacher can read it to them. The slip is returned to the bag, the child steps rung by rung forwards or backwards on the ladder according to his instruction, drops the bean-bag on the square on which he ends up, and returns to the back of his team. Then it is the turn of the next two children, who draw their instructions, go to the square marked by the bean-bag and pick it up, move backwards or forwards the prescribed number of steps, drop the bean-bag, and return to their team. The winning team is the one whose player reaches the end of the ladder first.

Stage I

Stage II

Stage III

Stage IV

Circle Time

Hall/PE

Literacy

Numeracy

Drama

Small Group

Art

Humanities

Science

DEVELOPING VOCABULARY

Make the Right Mark

Aim

To understand the terms 'tick', 'cross', 'join', 'ring', 'circle', as used in worksheet instructions.

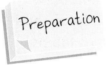

Equipment

A large sheet of paper, not less than A2. Drawing equipment – for example, felt pens or crayons.

Preparation

Using a thick black marker pen, draw as many triangles and squares as there are children in the group on the large sheet of paper. Either spread it out on a table or pin it up on the wall, so that it is clearly visible.

How to Play

Stand the children in a line, and give each child an instruction, using the vocabulary specified above. Each child then comes up to the large sheet of paper and makes the appropriate mark. Continue until everyone has had at least one turn. By the end of the game it should be clear which words are causing most difficulty to which children. Differentiated activities can then be set up to target those particular words.

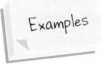

Examples

Tick a square, put a cross on a triangle, join two triangles, ring one of the squares, circle a square, etc.

Speechmark Ⓟ This page may be photocopied for instructional use only. *Speaking, Listening & Understanding*

DEVELOPING VOCABULARY

	Stage I
	Stage II
	Stage III
	Stage IV
	Circle Time
	Hall/PE
	Literacy
	Numeracy
	Drama
	Small Group
	Art
	Humanities
	Science

Counter Thief

Aim
To understand the terms 'first', 'second', 'third', and up to 'tenth' or 'last'.

Equipment

Counters, cubes or small toys.
A piece of cloth to conceal the counters.

How to Play

This is a game for a small group, not exceeding six children. The children should all be seated facing the same direction. Arrange 10 counters in a line so that they are clearly visible, counting them as you do so. Make sure the counters are well spaced. Once you have laid them out, ask the children to count them out loud as you point to each one. Now see if anyone can show you the first counter and the last counter. This will establish that they are counting from left to right. Tell the children there is a 'counter thief' about, and while their eyes are shut he will steal one of the counters. Ask them to shut their eyes, and as a precaution cover the counters with a cloth, as someone is sure to peep. Remove one of the counters, then take away the cloth and tell the children to open their eyes. Which counter has been removed? At first the children will need to be encouraged to give an ordinal number, rather than, for instance, the colour of the counter.

Tip

You may need to start with just five counters.

Extension

The number of counters can be increased as the children gain confidence in dealing with higher numbers.

Stage I

Stage II

Stage III

Stage IV

Circle Time

Hall/PE

Literacy

Numeracy

Drama

Small Group

Art

Humanities

Science

DEVELOPING VOCABULARY

Musical Measuring

Aim
To be able to understand the words 'more' and 'less', 'different and 'same as'.

Equipment

Enough identical glasses for the members of the group to have one each.
A metal knife or spoon, and a jug.
Access to water.

How to Play

This game is best played with a group of not more than six or so. Gather the children round the sink or water tray. Give each child a glass. Let them take turns to put some water in their glass. Explain as things go along that you want all the glasses to have a different amount of water in them, some more, and some less.
When all the glasses have some water in them, tap them in turn with the knife or spoon and show the children that they make different musical tones. Then help the children to arrange the glasses in a line, using the 'more' and 'less' criterion. When the glasses are arranged in order, let the children take turns to play a scale on them.

Extension

Do the same game, using 'higher' and 'lower' as a criterion.

DEVELOPING
VOCABULARY

Stage I

Stage II

Stage III

Stage IV

Circle Time

Hall/PE

Literacy

Numeracy

Drama

Small Group

Art

Humanities

Science

Tunnel Trap

Aim
To be able to understand the words 'through,' 'opposite,' 'apart' and 'between'.

Equipment

None.

How to Play

This game is adapted from 'Oranges and Lemons'. The children are organised into two lines facing each other, each child holding hands with their opposite number with raised arms, so that a tunnel is formed. During the organisation of the tunnel there is frequent opportunity for the adult to use the target words 'opposite' and 'apart'. (Stand *opposite* a partner in the other line. Stand far enough *apart* for people to get *between* you. Hold hands with your partner, with your arms up in the air. You've made a tunnel.) Now explain that the pairs are going to run *through* the tunnel in turns. They have as long as it takes you to count to five. If they are still in the tunnel when you finish counting, the children on either side drop their arms and catch them. They are then out. If they get through before you finish counting, they have escaped and join on to the end of the tunnel. The next pair then starts off. You can slow down your counting as necessary, to ensure that less confident children get through the tunnel safely, or speed it up to bring the game to a close.

Stage I

Stage II

Stage III

Stage IV

Circle Time

Hall/PE

Literacy

Numeracy

Drama

Small Group

Art

Humanities

Science

DEVELOPING VOCABULARY

Bizzo's Journey

Aim
To understand positional vocabulary: 'past', 'over', 'between', 'across' and 'middle'.

Equipment

'Bizzo's World' template from Teaching Resources, photocopied for each child.
Pencils.

How to Play

Tell the children that they need to help Bizzo make a path from the tree to his cottage. Tell them to put their finger on the tree at the top of the page. Explain that you will read them the instructions twice. The first time they must just listen carefully. The second time they will need to listen and draw the route with a pencil.

'Bizzo was standing by the tree. He was looking forward to going home and having a cup of hot chocolate and a peanut butter and jam sandwich. He walked past the pond. (PAUSE) Then he climbed over the gate (PAUSE) into the field. He walked across the middle of the field. (PAUSE) He stopped for a little rest, then climbed over the other gate. (PAUSE) It was a lovely sunny day and he could hear birds singing in the trees. He walked between the trees, (PAUSE) over the hill, (PAUSE) under the bridge (PAUSE) and into his own front garden.'

DEVELOPING VOCABULARY

Stage I

Stage II

Stage III

Stage IV

Circle Time

Hall/PE

Literacy

Numeracy

Drama

Small Group

Art

Humanities

Science

Pair Up

Aim
To be able to find your 'pair' by asking questions using the words 'number,' 'same' and 'pair'.

Equipment

Pieces of paper or card with large, bold numbers written on them. Sellotape or other means of sticking the numbers on the children's backs.

How to Play

Divide the children into two groups. Each child has a number stuck on their back, which they do not know. There should be two of each number – two ones, two twos, and so on. Explain to the children that they are at a party and have to find the 'pair' that they will be sitting next to. They will have to ask each other what number is on their own back, and then question each other further to find the child with the same number. When two children have come together as a pair, they go to the side of the room and sit down until all the pairs have been formed.

Extension

Write the numbers in colour so that there are now, for example, two red 'ones' and two blue 'ones', two red 'twos' and two blue 'twos'. The children will then have to extend their questioning.
Make it still more difficult by adding a symbol (eg, a flower or a balloon) so that the pairs have to match colour, number and symbol.

Stage I

Stage II

Stage III

Stage IV

Circle Time

Hall/PE

Literacy

Numeracy

Drama

Small Group

Art

Humanities

Science

DEVELOPING VOCABULARY

Categories

Aim
To be able to understand familiar category labels and think of items in a specific category.

Equipment

An object to pass around the circle.

How to Play

The children should be seated in a circle. One child is chosen to start the game. It is best to choose someone confident at this stage. They stand in the centre of the circle with their eyes shut. The object is passed silently around the circle until the child in the centre says 'Stop!' They then ask the child with the object to think of three items in a category of their choosing. That child then takes his place in the centre, and the object is passed around once more. Continue in this way until everyone has had a turn at being in the centre.

Examples of Categories

Food, animals, buildings, transport, sports, TV programmes, liquids, types of weather, careers, colours, dinosaurs, films, jewellery, clothes, and family members.

Tip

You may need to model this activity first. If possible, this should be done by the adults – one in the centre, the other with the object. However, it can be demonstrated by one adult, who can give examples of suitable categories. If a child is struggling to think of a category, you may need to suggest some for them to choose from.

DEVELOPING VOCABULARY

Stage I

Stage II

Stage III

Stage IV

Circle Time

Hall/PE

Literacy

Numeracy

Drama

Small Group

Art

Humanities

Science

Ready, Steady, Colour!

Aim
To understand the terms 'complete', 'shade', 'colour' and 'fill in' when applied to pencil and paper tasks.

Copies of the 'Ready, Steady, Colour' template and instructions from Teaching Resources.
Suitable colouring equipment.
A whistle or other noise-maker to indicate stop or go.

Make a copy of the template for each child. Arrange the sheets around one or two tables, depending on the size of the group. Put the colouring equipment on the tables.

Seat the children around the tables and explain that they are going to have a colouring race. They must not do anything until they hear the whistle. Give the first instruction, blow the whistle and wait while the children respond. When everyone has finished, blow the whistle to indicate that they should stop. Each child then passes the sheet of paper in front of them to the next person. Repeat until all the instructions have been given. Now it is time to check all the instructions have been carried out correctly. Each child checks the sheet in front of them, according to the criteria on the instruction sheet, which you read out. Points may be allocated for number of instructions followed correctly.

The game can be made more competitive by having two teams, one on each table.

Stage I

Stage II

Stage III

Stage IV

Circle Time

Hall/PE

Literacy

Numeracy

Drama

Small Group

Art

Humanities

Science

DEVELOPING VOCABULARY

Sort It Out

Aim

To understand the terms 'too many', 'not enough', 'about the same as', 'a few more' and 'a few less'.

Two teddies or similar soft toys.
A supply of counters.

Introduce the teddies to the children – give each a name. Show them the counters and tell them that in this game they are not counters, but sweets. Now ask the children to turn their backs, while you give different quantities of 'sweets' to each teddy. Leave a further supply of counters available. The children are now allowed to turn round. Choose one child, and say, for example, 'Biff hasn't got enough sweets, can you sort it out?' The child should give more counters to Biff. Encourage the rest of the group to comment on whether the problem has been sorted out. Then repeat the activity, asking the children to turn around, rearranging the counters and making another statement. Choose a different child to sort it out. Continue until everyone has had a go.

'Bill has got too many sweets now. Biff needs a few more.'
'Biff has just about the same amount as Bill. I think Biff needs a few less.'
'Now Biff hasn't got enough.'

DEVELOPING VOCABULARY

Kaleidoscope

Aim
To be able to understand the words 'beside' (next to), 'in front', 'behind', 'start from' and 'complete'.

Equipment

Coloured pencils and large pieces of paper, or a flip chart, or a white- or blackboard.

How to Play

Tell the children that they are going to make 'living patterns' to match some you will show them. You are going to tell the children, in turn, where to stand. When you have them all in position, you will show them the pattern they have made. You may prefer to have some patterns already drawn, or to draw each one after the last child has taken their place. Choose the first child and place him in position, saying 'We'll *start from* here.' Then tell all the others in turn, 'So-and-so stand *next to* ...' (or 'beside' – use the terms interchangeably), or '*in front of* ...' or '*behind* ...', as appropriate. As you come to the last child to be positioned, talk about how this will '*complete*' the pattern. Now, if you have time, 'shake the kaleidoscope' by getting everyone to run around for a minute, and then make another pattern.

Examples

An easy one is a cross. Position the first child where you want the centre of the cross to be. This is child A. Child B is told to stand beside child A. child C can be told to stand either beside child B or beside child A, and so on. When one arm of the cross has enough children on it, you can start the other arm of the cross by positioning children in front of or behind child A. Other easy patterns:

Stage I
Stage II
Stage III
Stage IV
Circle Time
Hall/PE
Literacy
Numeracy
Drama
Small Group
Art
Humanities
Science

DEVELOPING VOCABULARY

Stage I

Stage II

Stage III

Stage IV

Circle Time

Hall/PE

Literacy

Numeracy

Drama

Small Group

Art

Humanities

Science

More or Less Footsteps

Aim

To understand the terms 'more than' and 'less than'.

Equipment

Number cards, and 'more than' and 'less than' cards from Teaching Resources.

How to Play

Shuffle the number cards and deal one card to each child. The cards are numbered between nought and 10, so there may be more than one child with the same number. Keep the remaining cards, and the 'more than' and 'less than' cards, in two separate piles. Explain to the children that they are going to play a new kind of 'Grandmother's Footsteps'. Clear enough space for the children to be able to move from the other end of the room to where you are standing. The children then line up at the other end of the room. The rule is that they can only move forward if their card matches what you say. Stand with your back to them, and take a card from each pack, for example

more than	9

Call out 'numbers more than nine'. The children with number 10 on their cards can move forward one step. Take another card from each pile, and repeat. Continue in this way until a child reaches you, and lets you know by tapping you on the back.

Tip

It will be much easier to manage this activity if you have more than one adult.

P

DEVELOPING VOCABULARY

Stage I

Stage II

Stage III

Stage IV

Circle Time

Hall/PE

Literacy

Numeracy

Drama

Small Group

Art

Humanities

Science

Leave One Out

Aim
To be able to understand the meaning of 'all except'.

Equipment

Template and instructions from Teaching Resources. Crayons or coloured pencils.

Preparation

Copy and cut out enough of the pattern strips to give one to each child. Each child should have as many boxes on his strip as he has letters in his name, so some strips will need to be shortened.

How to Play

Give the children their strips and coloured pencils or crayons. Explain that you are going to tell them which shapes to colour in, box by box. Start with the first box, and tell the children 'Colour in all the shapes except the circle.' When everybody has finished, go on to the next one, 'Colour in all the shapes except the square.' Keep going until everybody has completed their strip. When the colouring is finished, tell the children to put one letter of their name in each uncoloured shape, to make a small banner.

Tip

Adopt the shortened version of children's names if possible (eg, Chris for Christopher), as otherwise some children will be playing longer than others.

Stage I

Stage II

Stage III

Stage IV

Circle Time

Hall/PE

Literacy

Numeracy

Drama

Small Group

Art

Humanities

Science

DEVELOPING VOCABULARY

Bean-bag Race

Aim
To be able to understand the words 'choose', 'team', 'arrange', 'in order' and 'compare'.

Equipment

Two bean-bags.

How to Play

Explain to the children that they are going to have a kind of relay race, involving them balancing a bean-bag on their heads. Identify two team leaders, selecting confident and competent children as the first leaders to show the way. Get the leaders to *choose* their team members in turn until two equal teams have been selected. Now tell the team leaders that they are to *compare* their team members in terms of height, and line them up *in order*, either tallest to shortest or the other way round, as they please. This may involve standing people back to back, and may mean some people removing shoes. Give as much help as necessary. When the two teams are correctly lined up, make a mark or place a chair to show where they have to walk to; hand out a bean-bag to each team, and start the relay race. As each child reaches the 'end' marker, they can take the bean-bag off their head, return it to the next member in the team, and go and sit at the side.

DEVELOPING VOCABULARY

Stage I

Stage II

Stage III

Stage IV

Circle Time

Hall/PE

Literacy

Numeracy

Drama

Small Group

Art

Humanities

Science

Count Down

Aim
To be able to understand the words 'either', 'neither', 'both' and 'none'.

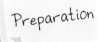

Equipment

Template and game instructions from Teaching Resources.

Preparation

Copy a sheet of shapes for each child and game instructions for you.

How to Play

Give the children a crayon each. Explain that they are to put a dot on the shapes as you call out your instructions. You will start with the shapes in Box 1, and work down line by line. Make sure everyone has identified Box 1, and have a short practice with the children pointing rather than marking their sheets. Once you are sure they know what they are doing, start calling out the instructions. Don't say 'Make a mark on', or 'put a dot on', simply say 'either of the…' or 'neither of the …', as indicated on the game instruction sheet. It may be necessary to say 'next line' as you move down. At the end of each box, ask the children to count up their dots. Have they got the right number?

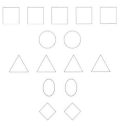

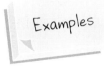

Examples

Put a dot on: All of the squares.
(Next line) Either of the circles.
None of the triangles.
Both of the ovals.

GETTING THE
MAIN IDEA

Stage I

Stage II

Stage III

Stage IV

Circle Time

Hall/PE

Literacy

Numeracy

Drama

Small Group

Art

Humanities

Science

GETTING THE MAIN IDEA

Story Spotter (1)

Aim
To be able to recognise key information in a sentence.

'Story Spotter1' template from Teaching Resources. 'Story Spotter1' sentences from Teaching Resources. Pencils or crayons.

Make a copy of the template for each child. There are eight sentences to choose from. You may want to cut the sheet into eight separate strips to avoid confusion. Alternatively, each child could put a blank piece of paper over all the rows except the relevant one. Tell the children to look at the four pictures in the relevant row. Tell them you are going to read out a sentence, and that one of the pictures will be important. They have to decide which is the important picture and mark it, by ticking or colouring in, etc.

Pictures: jumper, trousers, tree, toothbrush, boots
Sentence: 'It's pouring with rain, you will need your boots'.

GETTING THE MAIN IDEA

Stage I

Stage II

Stage III

Stage IV

Circle Time

Hall/PE

Literacy

Numeracy

Drama

Small Group

Art

Humanities

Science

Tick List (1)

Aim
To be able to listen for specific information.

Equipment

Counters.

Preparation

Choose three or four categories. Make a list of not more than 20 items, some from each category (see example below).

How to Play

Divide the children into groups to match the categories – for example, a group of animals, a group of food, a group of tools, etc. Give each child a supply of counters and a small container. Tell them you are going to read out a list of words. Each time they hear a word in 'their' category, they must put a counter in their container. When you have finished the list, get the children to count their counters. Have they got the right number?

Examples

Suggested categories: animals, food, clothes, buildings, transport, tools, sport.
Suggested list using animals, sport and clothes: dog, jumper, football, elephant, cow, socks, snooker, horse, tennis, trousers, hat, hamster, tie, hockey, rugby, sweatshirt, pig, coat, rat, swimming.

Stage I

Stage II

Stage III

Stage IV

Circle Time

Hall/PE

Literacy

Numeracy

Drama

Small Group

Art

Humanities

Science

GETTING THE MAIN IDEA

Story Points (1)

Aim
To be able to extract the key information from a story.

Equipment

'Story Points (1)' texts from Teaching Resources.
A4 sheets of paper divided into six sections, enough for each child in the group.
Pencils.

How to Play

Explain to the children that you are going to read them a story, and they need to listen carefully. Give out the A4 sheets and a supply of pencils. Tell them to number the boxes on the sheet, one to six. Then everyone must put down their pencil and listen while you read the story. Read the story, straight through, without pausing at the paragraph breaks. Then tell the children that you will read the story again, but in little chunks this time. At the end of each section they need to draw the most important parts of the story in the box on the sheet. Now read the first section. When you get to the end tell the children to draw the important parts in Section 1 on their sheet. Give them a short time to do this. Continue to read the other five sections in the same way. Now it is time to score the 'Story Points'. Go through each section, telling them how many points they could have scored. The winner is the child who scored the most points.

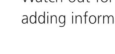
Tip

Watch out for cheats – you need to check no one is adding information while you are scoring the points!

GETTING THE MAIN IDEA

Stage I

Stage II

Stage III

Stage IV

Circle Time

Hall/PE

Literacy

Numeracy

Drama

Small Group

Art

Humanities

Science

True or False?

Aim
To understand a statement and judge whether it is true or not.

Equipment

Paper and pencils.

Preparation

Write down a list of statements, some of which are true, some which are not, as shown in the examples below.
Give each child a sheet of paper and a pencil.

How to Play

Explain that you are going to read out some sentences, one at a time. Some of the sentences will be true, some will not. Make sure everyone knows how to make a tick and a cross. They must put a tick on their sheet if they think the sentence is true, and a cross if they think it is false. At the end everyone checks their ticks and crosses, which should match the sentences on the list.

Examples

True
A spider is a mini-beast with eight legs.
It is important to brush your teeth at least twice a day.
A car will not go if it has no petrol in it.
Postman Pat's cat is called Jess.

False
Children go to school on Saturdays.
A worm has legs.
Bob the Builder lives on a ship.
Bicycles need petrol to make them go.

GETTING THE MAIN IDEA

Stage I

Stage II

Stage III

Stage IV

Circle Time

Hall/PE

Literacy

Numeracy

Drama

Small Group

Art

Humanities

Science

Titles (1)

Aim

To be able to match a suitable title to a short piece of text.

Texts available from Teaching Resources.

Write the relevant titles on to separate cards.

The children should be sitting around a table, or in a semicircle facing you. Give each child a title card, and then go around the group reading out each card. It is important that each child knows what is on his card. Then read a text and, if necessary, read it again. Now ask if anyone thinks they have the right title. If no one responds, go around the circle reading out each title and inviting the group to decide whether or not it is suitable. The child with the right title keeps the card. Play a further five rounds (or more if you wish). At the end, the winner is the child who has the most title cards.

Texts for some of the other activities in Teaching Resources could be used in the same way – they will need to be given a title if they do not already have one.

Speechmark ⑤ Ⓟ

GETTING THE MAIN IDEA

Story Spotter (2)

Aim
To be able to identify the key information in a known story.

Equipment

Fairy story picture sheets and scripts from Teaching Resources.
Pencils.

How to Play

Choose one of the fairy stories, and its script. Give each child a matching picture sheet and a pencil. Explain that you are going to read part of a story and that *some* of the pictures on the sheet will be in the story. Read the story once, with the children listening and looking at the pictures. Read the story a second time, asking the children to tick the pictures that you mention. When you have finished, go through the relevant items allowing one point for each correct item ticked.

Stage I

Stage II

Stage III

Stage IV

Circle Time

Hall/PE

Literacy

Numeracy

Drama

Small Group

Art

Humanities

Science

GETTING THE MAIN IDEA

Stage I

Stage II

Stage III

Stage IV

Circle Time

Hall/PE

Literacy

Numeracy

Drama

Small Group

Art

Humanities

Science

Story Points (2)

Aim

To be able to extract the key information from a story.

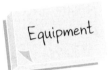

'Story Points (2)' texts from Teaching Resources.

Follow the instructions for Story Points (1). The only difference is that in this version the last part of the story has been omitted. Tell the children the writer didn't have time to finish the story, so they must think of their own ending. When they reach box number six, they will need to draw a suitable ending for the story. Add up the points as before, then ask each child to tell their own ending. Discussion can follow about which endings were best, most exciting, most interesting, etc. It is important that the ending relates to the rest of the story, and some children need help with achieving this.

The stories can be used for Literacy Hour word and sentence level work. The endings can be part of a creative writing task.

GETTING THE MAIN IDEA

Stories in Disguise

Aim
To be able to recognise a well-known story.

Equipment

'Stories in Disguise' texts from Teaching Resources.

How to Play

Tell the children you are going to read them a story. It is a story they have probably heard before, but it has been changed quite a lot and they will have to listen very carefully to work out which story it could be. No one is allowed to speak while you are reading, but as soon as someone thinks they know the story they put their hand up. Continue reading until the end, by which time nearly everyone should have their hand up. Then choose someone to tell you which story it is. Ask them how they managed to work it out.

Stage I

Stage II

Stage III

Stage IV

Circle Time

Hall/PE

Literacy

Numeracy

Drama

Small Group

Art

Humanities

Science

Stage I

Stage II

Stage III

Stage IV

Circle Time

Hall/PE

Literacy

Numeracy

Drama

Small Group

Art

Humanities

Science

GETTING THE MAIN IDEA

Hide and Seek

Aim
To extract key information from spoken language.

Equipment

None.

Preparation

This needs to be done while the children are out of the room. Select some personal belongings to 'lose' around the room. These could be: *'a watch', 'a comb', 'a small mirror', 'a pair of gloves, 'a pen', 'glasses', or 'a bracelet'*. Aim to hide one item for each member of the group to find. Unless you are very good at ad libbing, it is wise to jot down what you are going to say, perhaps using the example below.

How to Play

Tell the children you are having a very forgetful day, and you keep on losing things. Can they help you find them? The children should be seated around you while they listen to your description of when you last had the item. No one is allowed to speak until you have finished telling them. Anyone who thinks they know where it might be puts their hand up. When you have finished, choose someone with their hand up to go and look for the item.

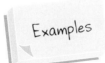
Examples

'I can't find my watch anywhere. I know I had it on this morning when I did the register. Then I took it off when I was cleaning the paint trays and I remember taking it over to the computer, ready for the Maths lesson.' (You will have put the watch by the computer.)

GETTING THE MAIN IDEA

Stage I

Stage II

Stage III

Stage IV

Circle Time

Hall/PE

Literacy

Numeracy

Drama

Small Group

Art

Humanities

Science

Tick List (2)

Aim

To be able to listen for specific information.

Equipment

Counters.
A small container for each child.

Preparation

Preparation

Choose three or four categories. Make a list of 20–30 items, chosen from those categories. Mix up the categories, as in the example below.

How to Play

This game is played in the same way as Tick List (1). It is a little more difficult, however, because the categories are very similar to each other. Divide the children into groups to match the categories – for example, a group of pets, a group of farm animals, and a group of wild animals. Give each child a supply of counters and a small container. Tell them you are going to read out a list of words. Each time they hear a word in 'their' category, they must put a counter in their container. When you have finished the list, they can check that they have the correct number of items.

Examples

Categories: farm, pets, wild animals
lion, tiger, rabbit, horse, guinea pig, sheep, dog, kitten, leopard, pig, elephant, hamster, cow, donkey, crocodile
Other closely linked categories:
fruit, vegetables, meat
clothes for PE, clothes for winter, clothes for summer
things that fly (birds, machines, insects)

GETTING THE MAIN IDEA

Story Spotter (3)

Aim

To be able to identify key information in an unknown story.

Equipment

'Story Spotter 3' template from Teaching Resources.
'Story Spotter 3' texts from Teaching Resources.

How to Play

This Story Spotter activity uses an unfamiliar text. Give each child a picture sheet and a pencil. Explain that you are going to read part of a story and that *some* of the pictures on the sheet will be in the story. Read the story once with the children listening and looking at the pictures. Read the story a second time, asking the children to tick the pictures that you mention. When you have finished, go through the relevant items allowing one point for each correct item ticked.

Sidebar navigation:
- Stage I
- Stage II
- Stage III
- Stage IV
- Circle Time
- Hall/PE
- Literacy
- Numeracy
- Drama
- Small Group
- Art
- Humanities
- Science

GETTING THE MAIN IDEA

Who's Got the Key?

Aim
To be able to identify the key information in a short story.

Equipment

Story texts from Teaching Resources.
The object that matches the chosen text.
Distracter objects.
A bag.

How to Play

The children sit in a semicircle facing you. Explain that you are going to give everyone something from the bag, but only one person will get the really important object, the 'key to the story'. Tell the children they need to do good listening and good sitting while you read them the story. They are not allowed to call out, put their hand up, or wave their object around while you are reading. When you have finished the story, you are going to ask who has the object which is really important in the story.

Tip

They may need to practise sitting quietly without fiddling with their object.

Extension

Pupils could draw a sequence of pictures to illustrate the story. More able pupils could write captions for their pictures.

Stage I

Stage II

Stage III

Stage IV

Circle Time

Hall/PE

Literacy

Numeracy

Drama

Small Group

Art

Humanities

Science

Stage I

Stage II

Stage III

Stage IV

Circle Time

Hall/PE

Literacy

Numeracy

Drama

Small Group

Art

Humanities

Science

GETTING THE MAIN IDEA

What's She on About?

Aim
To be able to work out the key information from a verbal explanation.

Equipment

'What's She on About' texts from Teaching Resources. Word lists written on sheets of paper.

How to Play

Tell the children that you are going to read them some non-fiction text. At the end you want them to choose what it is about, using the words on the sheet that goes with that particular text. Go through all the words before you start reading the text. If possible, use another adult to help demonstrate the activity. Read the text twice. Then hold up the relevant word list and read out the options. Ask the children if it was about A, B, C or D.

Example

'It is extremely important for children to learn how to cross the road safely. Lots of children are too busy playing or chatting to their friends to think about the traffic. They would rather be looking at their Pokemon cards, or playing on their Gameboys. Many accidents could be avoided if children knew more about the dangers of not paying attention to what is going on around them.'
Is this about: Pokemon, friends, road safety, or cars?

GETTING THE MAIN IDEA

Stage I

Stage II

Titles (2)

Stage III

Aim
To understand the main theme of a short text.

Stage IV

Titles (2) texts from Teaching Resources.

Circle Time

Hall/PE

This activity is similar to Titles (1), but is a little more difficult. This time the children have to listen to a short text and choose a suitable title from a list of three. Write the three alternatives on the whiteboard or a sheet of paper. Go through the possible titles before you read the text. No one is to call out while you are reading. When you have finished, read out the first title and ask for a show of hands. Note the number, then do the same with the remaining titles.

Literacy

Numeracy

Drama

Make the activity a little more difficult by concealing the titles until you have finished reading the text.

Small Group

Art

Humanities

Science

Stage I

Stage II

Stage III

Stage IV

Circle Time

Hall/PE

Literacy

Numeracy

Drama

Small Group

Art

Humanities

Science

GETTING THE MAIN IDEA

Jet Set

Aim
To be able to listen for specific information.

Equipment

None.

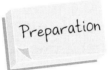

Preparation

Write some sentences containing the chosen destinations, as shown in the examples below. Write the names of the chosen destinations on cards.

How to Play

Choose a child to represent each destination. They should stand in different parts of the room, holding up their destination labels. Make sure everyone knows the name of each destination. The other children choose a partner and the pairs of children form a queue. Explain that you will be reading to them about the travels of a very rich film star who has their own private jet. The first pair must listen while you read the first sentence. They must not move until you have finished reading. They then have to move to the destinations mentioned, in the right order. If they are successful they win a 'jet point'.

Examples

1 He needed some shirts so he flew to LONDON to get them made.
2 Next day he flew to PARIS. The weather was cold and wet, so he decided to check out the jazz clubs in NEW YORK.
3 His best friend invited him to a concert in PARIS at the weekend. Then he had to be in LONDON for the premier of his latest film on Monday. After that it was back to PARIS for the French film awards.

GETTING THE MAIN IDEA

Story Spotter (4)

Aim

To listen to a short story and identify key elements.

Equipment

'Story Spotter 4' texts from Teaching Resources.
'Story Spotter' picture sheets from Teaching Resources.

How to Play

This is exactly the same as the earlier Story Spotter activities. However, at this stage there are more irrelevant items than relevant ones. This requires sharper listening skills on the part of the children.

Stage I

Stage II

Stage III

Stage IV

Circle Time

Hall/PE

Literacy

Numeracy

Drama

Small Group

Art

Humanities

Science

Speaking, Listening & Understanding
UNDERSTANDING SPOKEN LANGUAGE

THINKING SKILLS

Stage I

Stage II

Stage III

Stage IV

Circle Time

Hall/PE

Literacy

Numeracy

Drama

Small Group

Art

Humanities

Science

THINKING SKILLS

Password

Aim

To be able to use specific information to plan and execute a task.

Equipment

A small object to represent the 'treasure' – pretend coins or cubes are ideal.
A card with the location of the treasure written on it.

Preparation

Hide the 'treasure' item somewhere in the room. Then write where it is hidden on a small card. Choose a password.

How to Play

Tell the children they are on a desert island where there is some buried treasure. There is a giant on the island who is the guardian of the treasure. He knows where it is hidden, but he will only tell one person where it is – the person who knows the password. Choose a child to be the giant, and tell him what the password is, without the other children hearing. Give him the card with the treasure location on it. Now you need to tell each child a password. Give all the children but one the same password, which is incorrect. Give one child the correct password. Tell the children to stand in a line, ready to walk past the giant. Each child has to tell the giant his password. When the giant hears the correct password, he gives that child the treasure card. The child reads the card, with help if necessary, and if he can find the treasure, he keeps it. The game can be repeated several times.

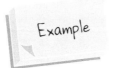

Example

Nine of the 10 children have *boots* as their password. The tenth has *wellies*.

THINKING SKILLS

Stage I
Stage II
Stage III
Stage IV
Circle Time
Hall/PE
Literacy
Numeracy
Drama
Small Group
Art
Humanities
Science

Space Words

Aim
To use familiar information to work out the meaning of an unknown word.

Equipment

A collection of about 10 familiar objects .
A puppet called Bizzo.
A list of nonsense words, one for each object.

How to Play

Introduce Bizzo, who comes from a distant planet. Tell the children that he has different words for the things on the table. Explain to them that they will be able to work out what the funny space words mean, if they listen carefully to what Bizzo says. You then read them Bizzo's sentences, as follows:

Examples

'I can't do my homework, I haven't got a wiffle.'
(Wiffle = pen.)
'It's freezing outside, where are my mimbles?'
(Mimbles = gloves.)

Stage I

Stage II

Stage III

Stage IV

Circle Time

Hall/PE

Literacy

Numeracy

Drama

Small Group

Art

Humanities

Science

THINKING SKILLS

Footprints (1)

Aim

To use thinking skills to work out a simple solution.

A set of prepared footprint outlines.

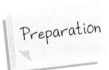

Make a master set of animal footprint outlines – for example, bird, elephant, horse, pig, lion, cat. Make a copy of the master.
Choose one of the animal prints, and make a trail of footprints across a large sheet of paper.

Show the children the copy of the set of animal footprints, and tell them which prints match which animal. Then explain that last night one of the animals escaped from the zoo and walked across the large piece of paper. Can they work out which animal it was?

Make trails using all the footprints, and ask which animals are in this zoo.

THINKING SKILLS

Looking and Thinking (1)

Aim
To be able to solve a simple problem by observing and thinking.

Equipment

Three containers such as cups or boxes.
A selection of small objects.

How to Play

Select three of the objects; show them to the children, and get the children to name them. Then ask everyone in the group to shut their eyes. Place one object under each container. Tell the children to open their eyes, and ask two volunteers to pick up a container each, revealing what is hidden underneath. Then ask a third child to tell you what must be under the third container.

Example

An eraser, a brick, and a stone.

Tip

Small children find it difficult to keep their eyes shut for long. Cover the table with a large cloth as a precaution against anyone peeping.

Extend the number of objects and containers.

Extension

Stage I

Stage II

Stage III

Stage IV

Circle Time

Hall/PE

Literacy

Numeracy

Drama

Small Group

Art

Humanities

Science

Stage I

Stage II

Stage III

Stage IV

Circle Time

Hall/PE

Literacy

Numeracy

Drama

Small Group

Art

Humanities

Science

THINKING SKILLS

Birthday Party

Aim
To be able to identify the nature of a task and organise a response.

Equipment

A worksheet for each child depicting an assortment of items suitable for a birthday tea, and several unsuitable items. (Photocopiable sheets are available in the Teaching Resources.)
Ten counters for each child.

How to Play

Give the children their worksheets and counters. Explain that Mum has bought lots of things ready for this birthday party, but she has had go off to work and has left the kitchen in a bit of a mess, and Uncle John in charge. Tell the children 'Use your counters to help Uncle John lay the table.' (You must use these exact words.) The children should place their counters on the pictures of jelly, cake, ice-cream and so on, leaving out the unsuitable items such as the medicine bottle, soap or toothpaste.

Extension

The same format could be used for other situations – for example, a trip to the beach or a day out in London. It is always important *not* to say 'Put your counters on the things we need', *but instead* 'Use your counters to show …'.

THINKING SKILLS

Stage I

Stage II

Stage III

Stage IV

Circle Time

Hall/PE

Literacy

Numeracy

Drama

Small Group

Art

Humanities

Science

Professions

Aim

To be able to select, from a choice, items that belong to particular professions.

Equipment

None.

How to Play

Choose a child to represent each of four different jobs. Position these 'workers' well apart from each other, at tables or around the room. Group the rest of the children together. Explain that you are going to call out a list of things. If one of the workers thinks that thing should be his, he puts his hand up. If he is right (eg, the policeman claims a police car), one of the children in the group is told to be a police car and go over to join him. If he is wrong, repeat the item until it is correctly claimed, and a child from the group goes to join the correct claimant. The game goes on until all the children from the starting group have joined one or other of the job groups. Then go around the jobs in turn, and see if all the children can remember what they were supposed to be. This is the moment to clarify the nature and use of items that some of the children may be unfamiliar with.

Examples

Policeman (police vehicle, helmet, whistle, handcuffs, badge).
Gardener (spade, fork, shears, lawnmower, wheelbarrow).
Cook (saucepan, wooden spoon, scales, butter, onions).
Doctor (thermometer, bandage, pills, ointment, syringe).

Tip

This game can be repeated as many times as you can think up different professions and the tools of their trade.

THINKING SKILLS

Next Please!

Aim
To be able to see the pattern in a sequence of shapes, and carry it on.

Equipment

None.

How to Play

Divide the children into two or more teams, giving each team a number. Write the numbers up on the board. Explain that you are going to draw some lines (sequences) of shapes on the board. They will make a pattern, and every time you stop drawing you are going to ask someone what they think should come next to carry that pattern on. You will choose people from each team in turn. When someone gets it wrong, or can't answer, pass the question on to the next team. For every correct answer, give that team a tick on the board. The winning team is the one with the most ticks when you stop.

Examples

✳ ☜ ✳ ☜ ✳

☐ ○ ☐ ○ ☐

○ ○ ☐ ○ ○ ☐ ○ ○

Tip

Make sure that the children are familiar with the names of any shapes you decide to use. Start with very simple patterns (eg, two alternating shapes) and gradually increase the difficulty.

Extension

Ask the children to justify their decisions. ('Because you've done two squares and then two circles, so now it should be two squares', and so on.)

Stage I

Stage II

Stage III

Stage IV

Circle Time

Hall/PE

Literacy

Numeracy

Drama

Small Group

Art

Humanities

Science

THINKING SKILLS

Stage I

Stage II

Stage III

Stage IV

Circle Time

Hall/PE

Literacy

Numeracy

Drama

Small Group

Art

Humanities

Science

Footprints (2)

Aim

To work out a solution from the information given.

Equipment

A collection of footwear of different sizes and designs.
A large sheet of paper.
Paint.

Preparation

Mix the paint quite thinly and pour into a tray big enough for the largest 'footprint'.
Select two different items of footwear and make some footprints on the large sheet of paper. Keep this sheet out of sight. Write a brief description of the owner of each item of footwear, and put their names on individual cards.

How to Play

Show the children the footwear, and tell them the descriptions of the 'owners'. Stick the names up on the whiteboard, or lay them out on a table so they are easily visible. Read through the names again. Now explain to the children that these characters are on holiday, by the sea. Last night two of them were out very late. Can they work out who they were, by identifying the footprints on the large sheet of paper?

Examples

Small child's shoe, belonging to Emma.
A large wellington boot, belonging to Dad.
A lady's shoe with a narrow heel, belonging to Auntie Sue.
A dog's paw print, belonging to Scruff. (This will have to be drawn.)
A bare footprint. (Either drawn freehand, or real!)

THINKING SKILLS

Stage I

Stage II

Stage III

Stage IV

Circle Time

Hall/PE

Literacy

Numeracy

Drama

Small Group

Art

Humanities

Science

New Clothes

Aim
To be able to work out how to arrive at a solution.

New Clothes templates and instructions from Teaching Resources.

Copy the sheets of dresses, one for each child. Copy the list of instructions for the teacher.

Give each child a sheet of the clothes pictures. Tell them that Mrs Fusspot is shopping for a dress She will turn down garment after garment. The children are to try to work out which garment will be bought in the end. When they have reduced the options down to one, will it be the right one?

Mrs Fusspot doesn't like silly bows. (Children should cross out all the dresses with bows.)
Mrs Fusspot says 'No checks thank you!' (Children should cross out all the checked dresses.)

This is a perfectly easy game if you *tell* the children how to eliminate one feature after another However, if you can, let them try to work out for themselves how to arrive at the right conclusion. You can try the game several times for them to try different tactics if they don't get it right straight away.

THINKING SKILLS

Stage I

Stage II

Stage III

Stage IV

Circle Time

Hall/PE

Literacy

Numeracy

Drama

Small Group

Art

Humanities

Science

Swift Solutions!

Aim

To be able to see and explain the solution to a simple problem fast.

Equipment

List of 'puzzles' in Teaching Resources.

How to Play

Get the children to line up in pairs. Explain that you are going to ask each pair in turn to solve a little puzzle, as fast as they can. If they can answer correctly, you will go on to the next pair. If not, they must run round to the end of the line so that they will get another question in a few minutes. 'Ready, Steady, Go!' Keep the pace as fast as possible.

Examples

'There aren't enough chairs around the birthday party table for everyone to sit down. What do we do?' (Answer: Get another chair/some more chairs.)
'The windows are open, its snowing outside, everyone is cold. What do we do? '(Answer: Shut the windows.)
'Mum's gone downstairs leaving the bath running. The water is nearly up to the top of the bath. What do we do?' (Turn off the taps.)
'Mum was feeding the parrot, but the phone rang and she went to answer it. She left the door of the cage open. What do we do?' (Shut the cage door.)

Tip

You will need to have a supply of similar puzzles at the ready. The object of the exercise is to elicit the obvious answer really quickly, though sometimes there may be some questioning (eg, 'Why would it be better to turn off the taps than shout for Mum?').

Stage I

Stage II

Stage III

Stage IV

Circle Time

Hall/PE

Literacy

Numeracy

Drama

Small Group

Art

Humanities

Science

THINKING SKILLS

Code Cracker

Aim
To understand a simple code.

Equipment

None.

Preparation

Each member of the group will need a number to represent his or her name. Choose no more than six easy actions – for example, close your eyes, stand up, clap your hands, stamp your feet. Each action needs a letter to represent it, see examples below. Draw a cartoon of the action and its letter beside it, on a large sheet of paper.

How to Play

Tell the children they are going to learn to understand a secret code. Give each member of the group a number, and spend some time making sure everyone is sure of their own number. This can be done by telling them to stand up when they hear their number. Now stick the sheet with the action pictures on it to the whiteboard. Go through each action, naming its letter. Choose a confident child to start the activity. Tell them what to do by saying their number and the letter of the action. If the right child does the correct action, they get a point. Once the children are familiar with the activity, you can name more than one child at a time, or more than one activity.

Example

Kelly (1), Sam (2), Jason (3), Zoe (4), Ranjit (5), Maria (6).
Clap your hands (X), Stamp your feet (Y), Close your eyes (Z), Stand up (Q)
3Y = Jason stamp your feet
6X = Maria clap your hands
4, 5Q = Zoe and Ranjit stand up

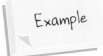

THINKING SKILLS

Stage I

Stage II

Stage III

Stage IV

Circle Time

Hall/PE

Literacy

Numeracy

Drama

Small Group

Art

Humanities

Science

First Things First

Aim
To be able to work out a logical sequence of actions in dealing with a problem situation.

Equipment

Scenarios from Teaching Resources.

How to Play

This game is best played with a group of not more than seven or eight, as with a larger group the discussion can take all day!
This is really a discussion group rather than a game, but you can liven it up by doing a bit of mime along the way. Select one of the scenarios and explain the situation to the children. 'What should they do first?' Having sorted that out, you ask 'What should they do next?', and so on, until the situation is resolved. You may have to remind them several times of the details of the situation.

Example

The boy has something in both his hands, and his dog has wound his lead around the boy's legs and around a tree. The bus is coming.

Extension

This discussion format could be used for real problem-solving.

Stage I

Stage II

Stage III

Stage IV

Circle Time

Hall/PE

Literacy

Numeracy

Drama

Small Group

Art

Humanities

Science

THINKING SKILLS

Clues

Aim

To be able to work out 'who dunnit' from known information.

Equipment

List of suspects and clues from Teaching Resources.

How to Play

Divide the children into two teams, and tell them that they are detectives. There has been a robbery and lots of precious jewels have been stolen. Three people have been spotted near the scene of the crime, and one clue has been left behind. You are going to tell them something about each of the three people who were seen, and you are going to tell them what the one clue is. Teams take turns to offer guesses. Keep going till they have had enough of it, or you run out of ideas!

Examples

A man smoking a pipe. A woman with a handbag. A boy on a bike. (Clue: Some ash on the floor.)

Tip

This game puts something of a load on memory. Be prepared to remind the detectives who the people are who were spotted near the scene.

Extension

Make one team the detectives, and enlist the second team to help you give the information they need. Where reading skills are adequate, you could give members of the second team the information in written form. Then swap teams.

Speechmark Ⓟ

THINKING SKILLS

Stage I

Stage II

Stage III

Stage IV

Circle Time

Hall/PE

Literacy

Numeracy

Drama

Small Group

Art

Humanities

Science

Bizzo

Aim

To be able to work out what an unknown word means by relating it to the context.

 **Equipment**

Text and word list from Teaching Resources.
Objects to match the chosen words.

 How to Play

Introduce Bizzo, the character from space, and explain that he doesn't speak very good English. Sometimes he forgets what we call things, so he uses his 'space' word instead. Bizzo is going to tell the children a little story, and they won't understand some of the words. Remind them that if they listen very carefully, and think very carefully, they will be able to work out what he means. Tell them not to call out, but to wait till you stop, and put their hands up if they think they know what the mystery words mean. Read one paragraph at a time.

 **Extension**

Write the words and their meanings. See if the children can use any of the words themselves in a meaningful sentence. Let them write or say a sentence for the rest of the group to interpret.

Stage I

Stage II

Stage III

Stage IV

Circle Time

Hall/PE

Literacy

Numeracy

Drama

Small Group

Art

Humanities

Science

THINKING SKILLS

Bus Driver

Aim
To be able to associate cause and effect.

Equipment

'Bus Driver' template in Teaching Resources.

Preparation

Make several copies of the 'Bus Driver' pictures.
Cut out the pictures.

How to Play

This game is for a small group, not more than 10. Shuffle the pack of pictures and put them in the middle of the table. The children are the drivers of buses, and they are to take turns to pick up a card. If a child picks a card picturing the bus only, their bus is on time and they keep the card. If they pick a card showing a potential problem, they have to work out and explain why their bus may be late. Their card goes back into the bottom of the pile. At the end, the child with the greatest number of 'bus only' cards in front of him is the winner of the 'best driver' award.

Examples

There is a flock of sheep around the next corner.
The bus has a puncture.
There is a level crossing around the corner and the barrier is closing.

THINKING SKILLS

Stage I

Stage II

Stage III

Stage IV

Circle Time

Hall/PE

Literacy

Numeracy

Drama

Small Group

Art

Humanities

Science

Weird Words

Aim

To work out the meaning of invented words by a process of elimination.

Equipment

None.

How to Play

Tell the children they are going to learn some words of a very strange language. You are not going to tell them what the words mean, they are going to have to work it out from what you do. Read out the first nonsense word, repeating it several times, and get the children to practise saying it. Then go round the room pointing at boys and girls in *random* order (not alternately). Point to a girl first, saying 'lally', then point to a boy saying 'banzer', and so on, occasionally pointing to a chair and saying 'seddle'. As soon as someone thinks they know what 'banzer' means, they should put their hand up . If they are right, go on to another word. If they are wrong, continue the pointing until someone has guessed correctly.

Examples

Target word: banzer (boy). Distracter words: lally (girl), seddle (chair).
Target word: scripple (book). Distracter words: blad (table), crump (pencil).

Tip

You can invent any number of these, but it is extraordinarily difficult to remember the words you have invented. So it is worth jotting them down with their meanings on a piece of paper.

Extension

Increase the number of distracter words.
The task becomes much more difficult if you progress to abstract words – for example, colours. Make sure there are plenty of objects in the target colour.

DRAWING INFERENCE

Stage I

Stage II

Stage III

Stage IV

Circle Time

Hall/PE

Literacy

Numeracy

Drama

Small Group

Art

Humanities

Science

DRAWING INFERENCE

Checkout Chat

Aim
To be able to use inference skills to decide which items belong to which character.

Equipment

'Checkout Chat' template from Teaching Resources.

Preparation

Make an enlarged copy of the picture template.

How to Play

Go through the shopping items in the picture, so that the children know what each item is. Then tell them you have overheard some people in the checkout queue at the supermarket. You are going to read out the things you overheard. The children have to try to decide which item belongs to which character. You can make the activity competitive by awarding points.

Text
Mrs White said 'I couldn't put the washing out until I'd got these.'
Mrs Green said 'I think Gemma eats it instead of putting it on the brush.'
Mr Black said 'I hadn't got any to put on my cornflakes.'
Mr Brown said 'I couldn't find any strawberries but I got all the others.'
Mrs Jones said 'It's Zoe's birthday tomorrow, she's going to be five.'
Lee said 'Dad finished the last packet yesterday.'

DRAWING INFERENCE

| Stage I |
| Stage II |
| Stage III |
| Stage IV |
| Circle Time |
| Hall/PE |
| Literacy |
| Numeracy |
| Drama |
| Small Group |
| Art |
| Humanities |
| Science |

Last Words

Aim

To be able to assign appropriate emotions to a situation.

Equipment

List of situations from Teaching Resources.

How to Play

Make a copy of the situations list. Divide the children into small groups. Explain that you are going to tell them about a boy called Charlie. Charlie finds himself in all sorts of different situations. You are going to give each group in turn the chance to finish off what you say. They will have to think hard how Charlie might be feeling. A group may produce several 'Last Words' at more or less the same time, calling out across each other. You will have to help them sort out which one they think is the best. Then say the sentence again, so that the whole group can say the 'Last Word' in unison.

Examples

'Charlie has been stealing some apples from Farmer Brown's apple tree. He is still up the tree when he hears Farmer Brown coming. *Charlie feels... .*'
'Charlie is waiting outside Father Christmas's grotto. *Charlie feels... .*'

Tip

This game is a preparation for the more difficult inference game, 'I Wonder', so discussion should be encouraged, and new words suggested by the teacher where appropriate or necessary.

DRAWING INFERENCE

Stage I
Stage II
Stage III
Stage IV
Circle Time
Hall/PE
Literacy
Numeracy
Drama
Small Group
Art
Humanities
Science

Think About It

Aim
To be able to answer indirect questions about a short text.

'Think About It' texts from Teaching Resources.
A whiteboard on which to record the team points.

Divide the group into two teams, A and B. Explain that you are going to read a short story, and then choose one of the teams to answer some questions. Remind the children to listen carefully, because some of the answers are 'hidden'. Then read the first story and select team A or B to answer the questions. If they are unable to answer, offer the question to the other team for a bonus point.

'Emma is in a shop with her mum. She has only one shoe on, and she is sitting on a chair. There are several boxes on the floor around her.'
'Where is Emma?'
'What is she doing?'

DRAWING INFERENCE

Stage I

Stage II

Stage III

Stage IV

Circle Time

Hall/PE

Literacy

Numeracy

Drama

Small Group

Art

Humanities

Science

Riddle Race

Aim

To be able to interpret simple riddles.

Equipment

A list of simple riddles from Teaching Resources. Counters.

How to Play

Divide the children into two teams. Each team starts with three counters. Ask the first child in team A the first riddle. If he gets it right, his team wins a counter. If he is wrong, his team loses a counter. Then ask the first member of the other team the next riddle. Continue until everyone has had a turn.

Example of riddles

'I'm made of metal, I can cut and you use me when you have your dinner.'

Extension

A timer could be used to add excitement. More riddles can be added to the existing list.

Stage I
Stage II
Stage III
Stage IV
Circle Time
Hall/PE
Literacy
Numeracy
Drama
Small Group
Art
Humanities
Science

DRAWING INFERENCE

Lost Property

Aim
To be able to match new information to known facts.

Pictures of the items in the 'lost property' box. Descriptions of people from Teaching Resources.

Show the children the cartoon pictures one at a time. Describe each person. Then take the items out of the box and lay them out so that everyone can see them. Select one item. Take the first 'person', and read the description again. Tell the children to put their hand up if they think they know who that item belongs to.

Possessions
Scarf, glove.

Characters
Josh's nan always knits him something for his birthday.
Old Mrs Trim gets very cold hands in the winter.

DRAWING INFERENCE

Stage I

Stage II

Stage III

Stage IV

Circle Time

Hall/PE

Literacy

Numeracy

Drama

Small Group

Art

Humanities

Science

Wacko's Wand

Aim

To be able to use inference skills to find a correct solution.

Equipment

Descriptions of characters from Teaching Resources.
A picture of Wacko's kitchen from Teaching Resources.
Paper and pencils for each child.

Preparation

Make a master set of pictures including one picture as original and six pictures with the wand blanked out. Each of the six pictures will have one 'clue' according to the intructions in the Teaching Resources.

How to Play

Explain to the children that Wacko the Wizard is in a very bad mood indeed because someone has stolen his wand. The last time he saw it was on the kitchen table, just before his friends came round to watch a video. Can they help work out who might have stolen the wand?
Next, read out the descriptions of Wacko's friends. Show them the picture of Wacko's kitchen, before and after the theft. Each picture after the theft will have a clue about the culprit. If anyone knows who the culprit might be, they must put up their hand to answer. They must also be able to justify why they have chosen that person. Make a note of any different answers, and then use a group discussion to reach a final answer. Repeat with a different character and clue picture.

Tip

You may only want to read two or three of the character descriptions.

DRAWING INFERENCE

Stage I

Stage II

Stage III

Stage IV

Circle Time

Hall/PE

Literacy

Numeracy

Drama

Small Group

Art

Humanities

Science

Weather Forecast

Aim

To be able to deduce the kind of weather expected, from what is said.

Equipment

Examples from Teaching Resources.

Preparation

Prepare for this game by getting the children to draw and colour some 'weather' pictures (snow, rain, thunderstorm, sunshine, wind, cloud). This could fit in with topic work or art. You want, as nearly as possible, to have the same number of pictures for each kind of weather.

How to Play

Choose the six pictures that best depict the different weather conditions, and put them on separate tables; or if playing where there is plenty of space, well apart on the floor. Ask the children to remember which kind of weather they drew, so that they know if they are snow people or sunshine people, and so on. You are going to give them some clues about what the weather is going to do. If they think it is going to snow, the snow people must go and gather around the snow picture. Similarly, if they think it is going to be sunny, the sun people must collect by their picture.

Examples

Dad said, 'My goodness, the sky looks dark. Time to get the sledge out of the garage.'
Mum said, 'Don't forget your hats and dark glasses if you are going to be out for a long time.'

DRAWING INFERENCE

Rover and the Vet

Aim
To be able to draw inference based on association of ideas.

Equipment

'Rover' picture sheets and texts from Teaching Resources.
Pencils.

Preparation

Copy the 'Rover' picture sheets, enough for each child to have one.
Copy the texts for yourself.

How to Play

Give the children a sheet of 'Rover' pictures each. Explain that these dogs have all been to the vet, and the vet has given their owners some advice. Read out one of the texts. Can the children work out which dog this applies to? 'Put a counter or make a mark on the dog you think it is.' Continue with the next text, and so on. Make sure you do not read out the texts in the order in which they appear on the sheet.

Examples

'Your dog needs to go on a diet.' (Very fat dog picture.)
'You need to give this dog some extra food.' (Very thin dog picture.)

Stage I

Stage II

Stage III

Stage IV

Circle Time

Hall/PE

Literacy

Numeracy

Drama

Small Group

Art

Humanities

Science

Stage I

Stage II

Stage III

Stage IV

Circle Time

Hall/PE

Literacy

Numeracy

Drama

Small Group

Art

Humanities

Science

DRAWING INFERENCE

Animal Lotto

Aim
To be able to identify animals from circumstantial evidence.

Equipment

Copies of Animal Lotto sheet from Teaching Resources, one for each group.
Crayons.
List of answers in order for teacher.

How to Play

Seat the children in small groups (not more than eight) around tables. Give each group an Animal Lotto sheet and a crayon. The sheets consist of eight boxes, each with four animals pictured inside it. Explain to the children that you are going to tell them some little 'stories' about the animals, but you are not going to say the animals' names. The children are going to take turns to guess which animal is in which story.
Identify one child in each group to go first. Explain that the first animal will be in the first box, and the child must make a mark on the right one. The Lotto sheet will then be passed on to their nextdoor neighbour, and the process repeated with the second box. When all the boxes have been marked, collect the Lotto sheets; check for doubtful or wrong answers, and discuss.

Examples

Box 1 (Dog/Cat/Horse/Fish). 'Bother that animal', said Mum, 'he left his bone lying about on the stairs again, and I nearly fell over it.'
Box 2 (Cat/Horse/Fish/Pig). 'You've forgotten to feed Percy again this morning', said Mum, 'he's hunting about at the bottom of the tank, and he can't find a scrap of food.'

Tip

You can repeat this game several times, using the same templates, by inventing different circumstantial evidence and thus identifying different animals.

DRAWING INFERENCE

Stage I

Stage II

Stage III

Stage IV

Circle Time

Hall/PE

Literacy

Numeracy

Drama

Small Group

Art

Humanities

Science

Dan's Day Out

Aim
To be able to understand a character's state of mind from a physical description.

Stories from Teaching Resources.

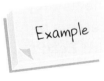

Tell the children you are going to read them a story. They have to guess from listening to the story how Dan is feeling… . If the children cannot come up with any reasonable ideas, offer three or four choices from 'happy', 'sad', 'excited', 'bored', 'scared', 'interested', 'sleepy', 'sick', and 'pleased', and ask who thinks that is how Dan is feeling. Hands up!

Example

Sample of Dan's Day Out text
Dan was going out for the day with his Mum and Dad. His eyes sparkled, and he sang a little song to himself as he ate his breakfast. ('How was he feeling? Do you think they are going somewhere nice, or not?' Sort out the suggestions, and then continue with the story.) They were going to a theme park where there were animals, rides, a playground, and a ghost train.

Stage I

Stage II

Stage III

Stage IV

Circle Time

Hall/PE

Literacy

Numeracy

Drama

Small Group

Art

Humanities

Science

DRAWING INFERENCE

Goody Goody!

Aim
To be able to understand implications.

Equipment

'Goody Goody' pictures from Teaching Resources.
'Goody Goody' storylines from Teaching Resources.

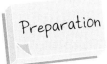
Preparation

Copy a sheet of the 'Goody Goody' pictures for each child, or for each small group if the children are working cooperatively.

How to Play

Give the individual children, or the small groups, a copy of the 'Goody Goody' pictures.
Explain that a lucky family has been given all sorts of amazing presents. The members of the family are all talking about the presents. The children must guess what the presents are, and put a counter or make a mark on the items they guess. Some of the pictures are not presents at all, and are just there to catch them out! Read out the clues, which can be in any order.

Example

Mum said, 'How lovely! Now we won't have to use the watering can.' (Hosepipe picture.)
Jo said, 'Yippee! Now I won't have to walk to school every morning.' (Bike picture.)

DRAWING INFERENCE

Stage I

Stage II

Stage III

Stage IV

Circle Time

Hall/PE

Literacy

Numeracy

Drama

Small Group

Art

Humanities

Science

Travel Agent

Aim
To be able to use indirect information to find a solution.

Equipment

Pictures of a variety of holiday destinations, taken from holiday brochures.
Descriptions of characters from Teaching Resources.

How to Play

If possible, stick the pictures on the whiteboard. Write the names of the characters on small cards. Tell the children that the travel agent's puppy got into the shop and muddled up all the names and holidays, and the travel agent cannot remember who is going where. Point out the pictures of the holiday destinations, but do not give much information about the types of holiday. Put the cards in a small box and seat the children around you in a semicircle. Let them take turns at choosing a name card from the box. Help them read the name if necessary. Then read out the descriptions of the characters, and see if the children can work out where each character is going for their holiday.

Stage I

Stage II

Stage III

Stage IV

Circle Time

Hall/PE

Literacy

Numeracy

Drama

Small Group

Art

Humanities

Science

DRAWING INFERENCE

Puppet in the Playground

Aim
To be able to make inferences from incomplete sentences.

Equipment

A puppet.
Picture Template and list of puppet's conversations from Teaching Resources.

Preparation

Make a copy of the picture sheet, and cut out the pictures. Copy the puppet's incomplete sentences, and cut them out for the teacher.

How to Play

This game is best played with a small group. Give each child one of the pictures. Tell the children that Pete the Puppet has been talking to people in the playground, and he is going to repeat little bits of his conversations. If a child thinks Pete is talking about the picture he is holding, he must show his picture. If he is right, he must try to explain what Pete the Puppet was talking about. If he is wrong, he puts the picture down again. If nobody makes the correct association with their picture, put the incomplete sentence to the bottom of your pile, and try it again later.

Examples

'…I think Sam pushed him.' (Goes with picture of child crying.)
'…lucky the pond wasn't very deep.' (Picture of dripping wet child.)
'… got caught up in a tree.' (Picture of child flying kite.)

Extension

Have two groups, and award marks so as to make the game a competition between them. (One mark for identifying the right picture, two marks for a good explanation of what the conversation was referring to.)

DRAWING INFERENCE

	Stage I
	Stage II
	Stage III
	Stage IV
	Circle Time
	Hall/PE
	Literacy
	Numeracy
	Drama
	Small Group
	Art
	Humanities
	Science

I Wonder

Aim
To be able to imagine a variety of possible reasons for a situation, and assign appropriate emotions to each.

Equipment

List of examples from Teaching Resources.

How to Play

Tell the children that you are going to have a competition with them. You are going to set some little scenes for them. If they can think of three or more possible reasons for each, they will have beaten you! They then have to decide how the character might be feeling in each of the different situations they have imagined. Play this game against the clock, giving the children 30 seconds to answer.

Examples

'Johnny is in the cupboard under the stairs.'
'Susie is running at top speed down the road.'

DRAWING INFERENCE

Stage I

Stage II

Stage III

Stage IV

Circle Time

Hall/PE

Literacy

Numeracy

Drama

Small Group

Art

Humanities

Science

Sixty-Second Stories

Aim
To be able to draw inferences based on the understanding of words such as 'again', 'as usual', and 'always'.

Equipment

'Sixty-Second Stories' from Teaching Resources.

How to Play

Explain to the children that you are going to tell them some tiny stories. At the end of each story, you are going to ask them a question. Sometimes the answer will be yes, and sometimes no. You will ask for hands up for yes, and then hands up for no. If a majority get the answer right, the class wins. If not, teacher wins! If you are playing this in the hall, or somewhere with plenty of space, you could have a 'yes' corner and a 'no' corner for the children to run to. This would make it easier for them to compare the number of yes answers and the number of no answers.

Example

'It was time to get up, but Sam snuggled down in bed and shut his eyes again. As usual, Mum had to come upstairs and pull the duvet off him. "You're going to be late for school again, Sam," she said. ''Haven't you been in enough trouble already?"' (Question: 'Do you think Sam has ever been late for school?' Answer: 'Yes'.)

Speechmark

DRAWING INFERENCE

Stage I

Stage II

Stage III

Stage IV

Circle Time

Hall/PE

Literacy

Numeracy

Drama

Small Group

Art

Humanities

Science

Find Fred!

Aim
To be able to deduce where Fred is from clues.

Equipment

Short scenarios from Teaching Resources.

How to Play

Divide the children into two or more groups. Explain that you are going to read them some little stories about a boy called Fred. There will be lots of clues to help them guess where Fred is. As soon as somebody thinks they know where Fred is, they must put their hand up. If they are right, their team gets a counter. If they are wrong, the next person to have put their hand up can try to answer. If nobody guesses right at this stage, continue the paragraph with more clues. When Fred's location has been guessed correctly, move on to the next story. The winning team is the one with the most counters at the end.

Example

'Fred sat by the window, staring out. It took some time for his eyes to get used to the dark outside. Suddenly, Fred nearly jumped out of his skin. Just outside the window was a huge fish, looking in at HIM! As Fred looked more closely, he could see other, smaller fish swimming about between the rocks and around the broken mast of the old ship. Then the engine noise got louder, and they zoomed away to find another wreck.'

Speaking, Listening & Understanding
USING SPOKEN LANGUAGE

DESCRIBING

Using Spoken Language

Stage I

Stage II

Stage III

Stage IV

Circle Time

Hall/PE

Literacy

Numeracy

Drama

Small Group

Art

Humanities

Science

DESCRIBING

Set the Scene

Aim
To be able to give the setting for a picture, identifying when it happened, and where it happened.

Equipment

None.

Preparation

Write down some scenarios (see examples below).

How to Play

Divide the class into two halves. Explain that you are going to make some 'pictures in their minds' by telling them about an imaginary picture. Then you will ask them some questions about it, asking the two halves of the class in turn.

Examples

1 'Lots of children wearing brightly coloured anoraks and bobble hats are tobogganing in the snow.' (Ask group 1: 'Is it summer or winter?' Ask group 2: 'Is it in the mountains or at the seaside?')

2 'A family is having a picnic. Some of the children are paddling, and some of them are making a sandcastle.' ('Is it summer or winter?', 'Are they at the seaside or in a railway station?')

3 'Some people are standing in a queue, carrying lots of bags and suitcases. There is an aeroplane taking off in the distance. The people are mostly wearing T-shirts and shorts, and some have sunglasses on. One child is eating a lollipop, and a baby is screaming.' ('Is it summer or winter?', 'Are they at the supermarket or the airport?')

Extension

When you give more detail, it becomes harder for the children to identify the essential background (as in example 3).

Speechmark

DESCRIBING

Stage I

Stage II

Stage III

Stage IV

Circle Time

Hall/PE

Literacy

Numeracy

Drama

Small Group

Art

Humanities

Science

Tell Me More

Aim

To be able to describe aspects of a composite picture.

Any pictures available in the classroom showing scenes in which several things are happening, the more detailed the better.

Divide the children into teams or groups. Hold up one of the pictures so that everyone can see it. Explain that the groups or teams are going to take turns to tell you something about the picture. The winning team or group is the one who can continue to think of something new to say after everyone else has dropped out. Just naming objects is not good enough!

A seaside picture. Contributions might be: 'It's the seaside', 'It's a nice day', 'There's a boat on the water', 'The children are getting ice-creams', 'A seagull is pinching a bit of sandwich', 'The dad has gone to sleep under his newspaper', or ' Somebody has made a sandcastle.'

Stage I

Stage II

Stage III

Stage IV

Circle Time

Hall/PE

Literacy

Numeracy

Drama

Small Group

Art

Humanities

Science

DESCRIBING

Guess What?

Aim
To be able to give a description of a familiar object.

Equipment

A collection of pictures of familiar objects.

How to Play

The children sit in a semicircle facing you. Start the game by selecting one of the object pictures and describing it without naming it. The first child to guess the picture comes and sits facing the group. Show them a different card without letting the rest of the group see. Make sure it is something they recognise. They then have to try to describe it without naming it. Carry on until everyone in the group has had a turn.

Examples

An orange: 'It's a fruit that is round, juicy and you need to peel it'.

Tip

Some children will need more prompts than others. Shy children who lack confidence could work in pairs.

DESCRIBING

Word Machine (1)

Aim
To be able to think of adjectives to match a target noun.

Equipment

An A4 sheet of card with a slit cut in it, large enough for picture cards to be posted through. You could label it 'Word Machine', and write 'Entrance' by the slit.
A one-minute timer.
Suitable pictures that can be posted.

How to Play

Child A chooses a picture of an object; puts it into the 'machine', and says what the picture is. Start the timer and write down all the adjectives that the children can think of in one minute. You can either go straight on to the next picture, or spend time discussing which words are best. This activity can be continued until time runs out.

Example

Target word: castle.
Suitable adjectives: old, ruined, forbidding, scary, enormous, and enchanted.

Tip

Another adult writes the words generated on a slip of paper, preferably unseen by the children. When the flow of adjectives dries up, put the slip in the 'machine', so that you can show the children what the Word Machine has produced!

Extension

Use the adjectives as a basis for word-level work.

| Stage I |
| Stage II |
| Stage III |
| Stage IV |
| Circle Time |
| Hall/PE |
| Literacy |
| Numeracy |
| Drama |
| Small Group |
| Art |
| Humanities |
| Science |

DESCRIBING

Stage I

Stage II

Stage III

Stage IV

Circle Time

Hall/PE

Literacy

Numeracy

Drama

Small Group

Art

Humanities

Science

Take Me There

Aim
To be able to describe an imaginary scene.

Equipment

None.

How to Play

Divide the class into two groups. Group One chooses a location from a choice that you offer them. Group Two then produces as many ideas as they can, in a given time, about this imaginary place. Depending on the composition of the group, you may wish to take 'hands up' for ideas, or let the children appoint a spokesperson and confer.

When the ideas are exhausted, or time is up, the groups change roles and Group Two chooses the location to be described.

Examples

A seaside somewhere hot. A goblin's cave. A farm. Father Christmas's workshop. A house in a tree. A factory making chocolates. A city under the sea.

Tip

Some prompting and indirect questioning may be necessary, particularly at first.

DESCRIBING

Stage I

Stage II

Stage III

Stage IV

Circle Time

Hall/PE

Literacy

Numeracy

Drama

Small Group

Art

Humanities

Science

Monster Collection

Aim

To be able to describe broadly similar pictures clearly enough to differentiate them.

Equipment

Monster Collection template from Teaching Resources. Pencils.

Preparation

Photocopy a set of monster sheets, enough for half the group. Photocopy an extra sheet and cut it up into individual cards.

How to Play

Divide the children into two teams, A and B, seated in lines opposite each other. The first child in Team A is given a monster sheet. Their opposite number in Team B is given a card matching one of the monsters. They hold it in their hand so that their opponent cannot see it. They must try to describe their monster so that their opposite number can guess which one it is. The 'guesser' eliminates groups of monsters that do not fit the description given, by crossing them out until only one is left. The monster sheet is then given to a child in Team B, while a Team A child has the individual card to describe, and the procedure is repeated. When a picture is guessed correctly, the 'describer's' team gets a point or a counter. The winning team is the one with the most points or counters at the end.

Example

'Its got curly hair.' (Guesser crosses out those with straight hair.)
'It's got long, wavy whiskers.' (Guesser crosses out those with short, stiff whiskers.)

Stage I

Stage II

Stage III

Stage IV

Circle Time

Hall/PE

Literacy

Numeracy

Drama

Small Group

Art

Humanities

Science

DESCRIBING

Who Can It Be?

Aim
To be able to describe a well-known story character for others to guess.

Equipment

A collection of well-known story books that the pupils will be familiar with.
Cards with the names of the characters on them.

How to Play

Allow the children to spend a little time looking at the books, and talking about the characters. Explain that no one is allowed to start guessing until three character clues have been given. Start the game off by describing a character yourself. The first child to guess correctly selects a new character card, and describes who it is. Continue until everyone in the group has had a turn.

Example

'She wears dirty ragged clothes, and has to do jobs for her horrible sisters.'

DESCRIBING

Stage I

Stage II

Stage III

Stage IV

Circle Time

Hall/PE

Literacy

Numeracy

Drama

Small Group

Art

Humanities

Science

Suspect!

Aim
To be able to ask a question using a complex sentence form.

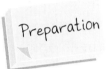

Equipment — 'Suspect' lotto board template from Teaching Resources. Deck of 'Suspect' cards made from lotto board template. Counters.

Preparation — Photocopy a lotto board for each member of the group. Use the template to make individual coloured cards of all the 'characters'. Colour all the hats in different colours.

How to Play — **Choose a child to take the Suspect card and hold it without anyone else seeing it. Give the other children a lotto board each. They then take turns to ask questions to try to find who the Suspect is by referring to the colour of the hat. For example, 'Is it the man with the red hat?' It is a good idea if you model the correct question form first. When the Suspect is discovered, each child covers that picture on their lotto board with a counter. Another child is now chosen to take a new Suspect card. You can make the game more difficult by colouring the hair as well. This will require a longer, more complex question.**

Stage I

Stage II

Stage III

Stage IV

Circle Time

Hall/PE

Literacy

Numeracy

Drama

Small Group

Art

Humanities

Science

DESCRIBING

Chickenpox

Aim
To be able to describe how someone might feel and look in certain circumstances.

Equipment

None.

How to Play

Announce that you are going to tell the children about some characters to whom various things have happened. The characters may feel sad or happy, ill or well, excited or afraid. When you have explained what has happened to a character, you are going to call out lots of words. Whenever a child thinks that one of the words fits the character in your little scenario, he must put his hand up. If you disagree, allow for discussion at this point. It can be a good idea to write down on the board or flip-chart all the describing words that are agreed upon. When you have a list of appropriate words for a character, recapitulate for the children by repeating them.

Examples

Johnnie has chickenpox. He looks (*spotty*, pretty, peculiar, extraordinary, lovely, *ill*, green). He feels (*sick*, well, happy, *hot*, cold, *unhappy*, *bored*).
Thomas the Tank Engine has just had a good wash, and is going out on a new track. He looks (dirty, muddy, shabby, *clean*, *shiny*), and he feels (*excited*, *scared*, cross, bored, angry, sleepy).

  Speechmark ⓢ ⓟ This page may be photocopied for instructional use only. *Speaking, Listening & Understanding*
© C Delamain & J Spring 2003

DESCRIBING

Word Machine (2)

Aim
To be able to generate verbs to match a target noun.

Equipment

The 'Word Machine', as used in Word Machine (1).
Pictures of familiar people or animals, cut out from magazines, etc.
Timer or stopwatch.

How to Play

Child A chooses a picture of an object; puts it into the 'machine', and says what the picture is. Start the timer and write down all the verbs that the children can think of in one minute. You can either go straight on to the next picture, or spend time discussing which words are best. This activity can be continued until time runs out.

Example

Target word: dog.
Verbs: barks, runs, bites, eats, sleeps, drinks, fights, scratches, chews, licks.

Stage I

Stage II

Stage III

Stage IV

Circle Time

Hall/PE

Literacy

Numeracy

Drama

Small Group

Art

Humanities

Science

Stage I

Stage II

Stage III

Stage IV

Circle Time

Hall/PE

Literacy

Numeracy

Drama

Small Group

Art

Humanities

Science

DESCRIBING

My Room

Aim
To be able to describe a room, giving appropriate details.

None.

Explain to the children that you are all going to take turns to describe the room you sleep in. The teacher has the first go, counting on fingers or marking on the blackboard how many different facts she can think of. Can any of the children beat that total?

After the game, ask the children to look very carefully at their bedrooms when they get home that evening, and warn them that you are going to play the game again the next day. Can they improve their descriptions?

Speechmark

DESCRIBING

Stage I

Stage II

Stage III

Stage IV

Circle Time

Hall/PE

Literacy

Numeracy

Drama

Small Group

Art

Humanities

Science

Where Am I?

Aim

To be able to give a description of a place.

Equipment

None.

Preparation

Write the names of different places on small cards. Examples might be inside a cave; at the swimming pool; on the beach; in a café, or at the top of a hill. You need a card for each member of the group.

How to Play

The cards are placed face down on the table. The first child chooses a card, without letting anyone else see it. Help him to read the 'location'. He then has to try to describe it, without saying where it is. The rest of the group listen to his description, and anyone who thinks he knows where it is, puts his hand up. No calling out is allowed. The first child to guess the location takes the next turn. Continue until everyone has had a turn.

Examples

In a cave. 'It's dark and the ground is wet. The walls are made of rock. It's scary and I can hear the sea.'

Tip

Take the first turn yourself, so that you can model the activity. Choose a confident child to start with. If a child is finding it difficult to give clues, you may need to ask some suitable questions to prompt a description.

Extension

The children could draw some of the locations, and they could be used as the basis for creative writing tasks.

DESCRIBING

Wacko's Week

Aim
To be able to describe a range of different activities.

Equipment
None.

Preparation
Write each day of the week at the top of seven separate sheets of paper.

How to Play
Tell the children that Wacko the Wizard is going to spend his week's holiday at home. He isn't very good at organising himself, and you want the children to help him plan his week. Start them off by taking the Monday sheet, and saying one thing that Wacko does on Monday morning. Choose a confident child to contribute another activity. When you have reached about six activities for that day, move on to the next. Try to encourage everyone in the group to add some information. After the children have become familiar with the activity, they will start competing for the funniest or most ridiculous things for Wacko to do.

Example
'On Monday morning Wacko woke up, and ate a jam and peanut butter sandwich in bed while he did the crossword in the Wizard Gazette.'

Extension
This activity could form the basis for creative writing work. The children could draw or paint pictures to go with the activities.

Stage I
Stage II
Stage III
Stage IV
Circle Time
Hall/PE
Literacy
Numeracy
Drama
Small Group
Art
Humanities
Science

DESCRIBING

Stage I

Stage II

Stage III

Stage IV

Circle Time

Hall/PE

Literacy

Numeracy

Drama

Small Group

Art

Humanities

Science

Journey Home

Aim

To be able to describe some of the things you see on your way home from school.

None.

Tell the children you are going to take turns to describe your journey from school to home. It doesn't matter whether you go by car, bus, taxi, bicycle or on foot. The teacher will have the first turn, and count on fingers or by marking on the board how many things they can remember seeing or doing on their journey. Can any of the children beat that total?

Example

You pass a letterbox and post a letter; you pass a specially pretty garden with tall sunflowers in it; you pass the Police Station and see a police car outside; you go under some big trees and pick up some conkers.

Tip

Ask the children to take special notice on their trips home that evening, as you will be playing the game again the next day and will see if they can improve their record.

Stage I

Stage II

Stage III

Stage IV

Circle Time

Hall/PE

Literacy

Numeracy

Drama

Small Group

Art

Humanities

Science

DESCRIBING

Film Directors

Aim

To be able to describe a simple scene, naming the characters involved and what they were doing.

Equipment

None.

How to Play

Divide the children into two groups. One group is going to provide the actors for some simple scenes. The other group is the audience, and the children in the audience turn their backs on the 'stage'. Choose one, two, or three children from the 'actors' group. Arrange them sitting, standing, on chairs or on the floor, in a circle, one behind the other, or however you decide. Then choose one of the actors to describe to the audience the scene you have arranged. When this is finished, disperse the actors; remove or rearrange the chairs if any were used, and tell the audience to turn around. Now choose one child from the audience to attempt to rearrange the scene as it was described. Allow for questioning, correction, and argument until the scene is arranged correctly.

Examples

Rebecca and Charlie are sitting on chairs facing each other.
Jamie, Debbie and Brett are sitting on the floor, in a line one behind the other.

Tip

Let the actor team have quite a few turns before you swap the teams over, otherwise it takes too long, and the children can become confused.

DESCRIBING

Stage I

Stage II

Stage III

Stage IV

Circle Time

Hall/PE

Literacy

Numeracy

Drama

Small Group

Art

Humanities

Science

Spiders' Webs

Aim
To be able to think of words of the same or similar meaning.

Equipment

Copies of the spiders' webs from Teaching Resources, enough for each team to have one.

How to Play

Divide the children into two or more teams. Each team chooses a 'scribe', who takes charge of his team's web. Explain to the children that you are going to call out a word, and then members of each team in turn will have a chance to come up with words of the same or broadly similar meaning. Whenever you agree with the chosen word, that team's scribe uses a crayon to colour in a segment of their web. If you disagree, move on to the next team. You are unlikely to get more than two, or at most three suitable suggestions for each word, so be prepared to start with a new word when you think it appropriate. The game is over when one team has a completely coloured web.

Example

Pretty (lovely, beautiful, gorgeous, ravishing).
Delicious (tasty, yummy, nice, good).
Horrible (nasty, beastly, unkind, cruel).
Frightening (scary, terrifying, horrible, alarming).

Extension

You can use the webs in a similar way to ask the teams to supply opposites (kind/cruel, beautiful/ugly, nice/nasty, good/bad, quick/slow), or to play a form of Free Association in which you give the children a word (eg, 'bonfire'), and ask them to produce words that they associate with it (smoke, flames, autumn, leaves, hot, crackling, Guy Fawkes, and so on).

After a game, let the children challenge *you* to produce some more words.

EXPLAINING

Stage I

Stage II

Stage III

Stage IV

Circle Time

Hall/PE

Literacy

Numeracy

Drama

Small Group

Art

Humanities

Science

EXPLAINING

Potty Pictures

Aim
To be able to explain what is wrong in a picture.

Equipment

Set of 'what's wrong' cards. (There are several packs available commercially, eg, ColorCards®.)
Blackboard and chalk, whiteboard and marker, or flip-chart and felt pen, for teacher.

How to Play

Children sit in a semicircle in front of the teacher. The first child is given one of the pictures, and asked to explain to the teacher what is wrong with it. The teacher attempts to draw what the child has told her. If the explanation is totally inadequate, invite another child (or 'hands up') to give further clarification, until you are able to reproduce a rough copy of the picture on the blackboard.

Examples

A bird flying upside down.
A dog walking half a metre above the ground.
A house with its front door upstairs.

Extension

Give the children turns to explain how you should put the picture right.

EXPLAINING

	Stage I
	Stage II
	Stage III
	Stage IV
	Circle Time
	Hall/PE
	Literacy
	Numeracy
	Drama
	Small Group
	Art
	Humanities
	Science

They Belong

Aim

To be able to see the connection between various objects, and explain it.

Equipment

'They Belong' template from Teaching Resources.

Preparation

Photocopy and cut out enough of the 'They Belong' card pairs for each child to have two turns.

How to Play

Deal out one card from each pair to the children. (Eg, the collar, but not the dog; the spider, but not the web; the cheese, but not the mouse.) Get the children to spread them out in front of them. The teacher keeps the picture pairs in her hand. Tell the children that you are going to turn up one of your cards at a time. If a child thinks the card 'goes with' one that he has, he calls out 'Me!' He then has to justify his claim. If his explanation is adequate, he gets the picture pair. If not, that pair goes into a reject pile. Continue until all the cards are used up.

Stage I
Stage II
Stage III
Stage IV
Circle Time
Hall/PE
Literacy
Numeracy
Drama
Small Group
Art
Humanities
Science

EXPLAINING

Sentence Builder

Aim
To be able to enhance a very simple sentence.

Equipment

A supply of blocks or cubes, which can be balanced on top of each other.

A list of very simple sentences (see examples below).

How to Play

Place one block in the middle of the table. Read out one of the sentences, and invite the children to try to add a bit to the sentence. When someone adds a bit, put a block on top of the first one. Continue in this way, aiming to build the sentence block as high as you can. If possible, record the sentences, either by writing them down, or using a tape recorder.

Examples

The car drove by. ('The red car drove by.' 'The red car drove by slowly… .')

My cat looked up. ('My black cat looked up.' 'My black cat looked up and yawned… .')

She picked a flower. ('She picked a yellow flower.' 'She picked a yellow flower in the garden … .')

It was Monday. ('It was a wet Monday.' 'It was a wet Monday in winter … .')

EXPLAINING

Stage I

Stage II

Stage III

Stage IV

Circle Time

Hall/PE

Literacy

Numeracy

Drama

Small Group

Art

Humanities

Science

Picture Grid

Aim

To be able to give a clear explanation.

Equipment

The 'Picture Grid' template from Teaching Resources. A sheet of paper for each child, divided into 10 equal boxes.

Preparation

Cut up the 'Picture Grid' into individual cards, shuffle and put in a pile face down.

How to Play

Ask the children to number the boxes from one to 10. Choose a child to start. He comes to the front of the class, and you show him the top picture on the pile. No one else may see it. He then has to tell everyone else exactly what to draw. If possible, let him draw it as well, but make sure no one can see it. He then returns to his place, and the next child comes and instructs the class according to the next picture. Continue in this way until everyone has had a turn. Compare the children's drawings with the 'Picture Grid' diagrams and discuss what they may have got wrong.

Extension

You can easily make additional pictures.

Example

A triangle inside a circle.

Stage I

Stage II

Stage III

Stage IV

Circle Time

Hall/PE

Literacy

Numeracy

Drama

Small Group

Art

Humanities

Science

EXPLAINING

Copycat

Aim

To be able to give accurate instructions to make a drawing.

Equipment

Paper and drawing equipment.
A screen or barrier for each pair of children.

Preparation

Pairs of children need a table each, where they sit facing each other with a barrier between them.

How to Play

Explain that the children are going to make some drawings and tell their partner exactly what they have drawn. The partner then draws what they are told, and at the end the two drawings are compared. The drawings that contain the same features (regardless of the standard of drawing) are the most successful. Each child should have the opportunity to both give and receive instructions.

Examples

The following examples may be chosen: a monster; a fantastic plant; a cottage in the woods; the kitchen table; fun in the snow; on the beach; Wendy the witch, or a car.

EXPLAINING

Stage I

Stage II

Stage III

Stage IV

Circle Time

Hall/PE

Literacy

Numeracy

Drama

Small Group

Art

Humanities

Science

Match Mine

Aim
To be able to give clear instructions for arranging objects to correspond to a simple picture.

Equipment

Toy tea set.
A toy apple and toy carrot.
Pictures from Teaching Resources, which are graded according to difficulty, photocopied and cut out.

How to Play

Divide the children into pairs. The first pair sit opposite each other at a small table, while the rest of the class or group form the audience. One member of the pair (Child A) is given a picture which he conceals from his partner (a screen in the middle of the table is best). The partner (Child B) has a range of items from a toy tea set, and some toy food. Explain that Child A has to tell Child B how to arrange his objects, so that they correspond with the picture. Give them a minute or two, then lift the screen and compare.

Examples

The picture shows a cup, and a plate with an apple on it.

Tip

This game can be adapted according to the availability of suitable toys. It can be played equally well using toy farm animals; dolls' house furniture and people, or toy vehicles and buildings. If any of these are used, quick sketches can be made of simple arrangements. Alternatively, the pairs may be given matching sets of toys; Child A can arrange his set as he wishes, instead of a picture.

When the two scenarios do not match, it is important to discuss with the children what went wrong. What was not clearly explained, or what was not understood?

Stage I

Stage II

Stage III

Stage IV

Circle Time

Hall/PE

Literacy

Numeracy

Drama

Small Group

Art

Humanities

Science

EXPLAINING

What on Earth is This?

Aim
To be able to give a simple definition.

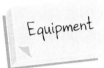

Pictures of everyday objects – see examples below. Some sort of puppet to represent an alien visitor.

Explain to the children that Bizzo, the visitor from 'out there' is having trouble working out what things are for. Point out the pictures on the table. Ask them if they would be able to tell Bizzo some important information about each item. Then give them an example: pick up the picture of the hammer, and say 'This is called a hammer. A hammer is a tool for banging in nails.' Then pick up another object, and encourage the children to think up their own definitions.

A hammer, supermarket, burger, car, bed, or jumper. (These represent tools, buildings, food, transport, furniture, and clothes.)

EXPLAINING

Stage I

Stage II

Stage III

Stage IV

Circle Time

Hall/PE

Literacy

Numeracy

Drama

Small Group

Art

Humanities

Science

Claim It

Aim
To be able to recognise items belonging to the same category, and explain the relationship.

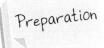

Equipment

'Claim It' cards from Teaching Resources.

Preparation

Photocopy and cut out enough of the 'Claim It' cards for the number of children playing. Colour the cards if possible. For example, if five children are playing, you will need to include five categories (say food, transport, clothing, furniture, and animals) and four or more items in each category.

How to Play

This game is best played with a small group, not more than five or six children. Give each child a card, representing different categories (one food item, one transport item, and so on). The adult holds the remaining pack. Explain to the children that you are going to turn up one card at a time from your pack. If a child thinks it belongs to his category, he calls out 'Me'. He then has to justify his claim by explaining that it is 'food' or 'an animal', and if able to do so, he gets the card. If his explanation is inadequate or incorrect, the card goes back into the teacher's pack. Stop the game when everyone has had the same number of turns, but while there are still some cards in your hand. The winner is the child who has the most cards.

Tip

The game can be played non-competitively by allowing it to continue until all the cards have been claimed. If the children are still very unsure of the category names, you can play the game at first by allowing explanations such as 'they live on a farm', or 'you can eat it', while using the category names yourself.

EXPLAINING

Stage I

Stage II

Stage III

Stage IV

Circle Time

Hall/PE

Literacy

Numeracy

Drama

Small Group

Art

Humanities

Science

Because!

Aim

To be able to think of and explain possible reasons for situations described.

Equipment

'Because!' texts from Teaching Resources.

How to Play

Have the children seated in a circle. A small group (not more than seven or eight) is best for this game. Tell the children that you are going to describe a situation. Everyone, in turn, has to try to think up a reason for it. The target is five reasons. If the group reaches five reasons, the teacher claps hands, or bangs a drum, or blows a whistle. The aim of the game is to beat the target more times than not – for example, to beat the target four times out of seven.

Examples

A child crying by a bus stop. (Possible reasons: They missed the bus; lost the money for their fare; forgot their destination, feel frightened travelling on their own; have been teased or bullied by older children; feel cold; can't remember the number bus they need, or have got a tummy ache.)

Tip

This can be made rather like a typical TV contest show.

Speechmark

EXPLAINING

Category Circle

Aim
To be able to explain why two items go together.

Equipment

A collection of familiar objects, see examples below.

How to Play

The children need to sit on the floor in a circle. The objects are placed in a group in the middle. There needs to be enough space to make a circle with the objects. Ask one child to choose something from the collection of objects and place it in front of them. You then choose another item, place it beside the first item, and say why those two things can go together. The child next to you then has a go. They can match their object to either of those already in position. Any object may be chosen, as long as the child can say why it goes with its next-door neighbour. The aim is to make a complete circle, but this is not always possible.

Examples

Objects in group
Ruler, pencil, book, plastic cube, apple, ball, plant, cup, glove, scarf, paint brush, gluestick, tissue, marble, magnifying glass, scissors, rubber, mirror, skipping rope
Putting them together
ruler + plastic cube (they are both plastic)
plastic cube + glove (they are both red)
glove + scarf (both keep you warm)
scarf + skipping rope (both long)

Stage I

Stage II

Stage III

Stage IV

Circle Time

Hall/PE

Literacy

Numeracy

Drama

Small Group

Art

Humanities

Science

EXPLAINING

Stage I

Stage II

Stage III

Stage IV

Circle Time

Hall/PE

Literacy

Numeracy

Drama

Small Group

Art

Humanities

Science

Consequences

Aim
To be able to give an accurate instruction.

None.

You will need to draw a figure (a person, animal or monster) on a sheet of A4 paper.
You then need a long strip of paper, or several sheets joined together, see example below.

How to Play

Divide the group into two teams, A and B. Choose a child from Team A to give the instruction, and a child from Team B to start the drawing. Show the child from Team A the head section of your picture. No one else must see it. He tells the child from Team B exactly what to draw. When he has done his drawing, he folds over the top of the strip, so that only a little bit of the neck is visible. He then passes the strip to Team A. This time, show the child from team B the next bit of the picture. He describes this for a member of Team A to draw. Continue like this, swapping teams, until the drawing is finished. You can then have great fun comparing the children's version with the original.

EXPLAINING

Stage I

Stage II

Stage III

Stage IV

Circle Time

Hall/PE

Literacy

Numeracy

Drama

Small Group

Art

Humanities

Science

Late Again!

Aim
To be able to think of, and explain, possible reasons for being late for school.

Equipment

None.

How to Play

Tell the children that you have an imaginary friend who is always being late for school. He has a different reason for every day of the school week. Can the group think of five different reasons he might give? 'Hands up!' If they can find five or more, they've beaten him.

Examples

He overslept. His school clothes were still in the wash. The bus was early. Mum burnt the breakfast and had to make some more. He couldn't find one of his shoes. He had a quarrel with his sister or brother. He had to clean out the guinea pig's cage. The budgie was sick and had to be taken to the vet.

Extension

Offer other scenarios, for example: Why did somebody miss his aeroplane? Why did somebody not turn up for his dentist's appointment? Why did somebody go out wearing one black and one brown shoe? Why was somebody sitting on the beach on a lovely sunny day with a thick coat on?

If the children get good at this, try dividing them into two teams. Take suggestions from each team alternately, and see which team can go on producing ideas the longest.

EXPLAINING

Stage I

Stage II

Stage III

Stage IV

Circle Time

Hall/PE

Literacy

Numeracy

Drama

Small Group

Art

Humanities

Science

Martian Meals

Aim

To be able to explain how to make a simple meal.

Equipment

Toy food and toy tea-set and kitchen equipment; real ingredients; playdough items, or any combination of these.

How to Play

This game has most impact if played with real ingredients and kitchen equipment, and could be carried out at the start of a cookery activity. Choose one child to be 'teacher' and a second child to be the 'Martian' The rest of the group can watch as other Martians. Explain that Martians have never come across a jam sandwich, and the 'teacher' is going to tell the Martian how to go about preparing one. The 'teacher' then attempts to instruct the 'Martian', who should follow the directions exactly. When things go wrong, the 'teacher' should be encouraged to correct her instructions.

Examples

A jam sandwich, a biscuit, jam tarts, a boiled egg, a cup of tea, or a bowl of cereal.

Tip

Both 'teacher' and 'Martian' may need some help with this activity, particularly the first time it is played. It may be necessary for the real teacher to take the part of the Martian until the children get the idea.

EXPLAINING

Stage I

Stage II

Stage III

Stage IV

Circle Time

Hall/PE

Literacy

Numeracy

Drama

Small Group

Art

Humanities

Science

Not Like That!

Aim
To be able to explain the rules and procedures of a simple game.

Equipment

Snakes and Ladders board, counters and die.

How to Play

This game is best played with a small group. Choose one child out of the group, and seat the rest of the children around the table so that they can see clearly what is going on. Teacher and child have the Snakes and Ladders board between them. The teacher explains that she has 'never played this game before', and the child has to tell her what she has to do. Follow the child's instructions exactly. If this results in the teacher doing the wrong thing, or a complete muddle, choose another child from the group who thinks he can sort things out. The children now take turns to tell the teacher the next steps in the game. Prompt if necessary with 'What do I do next?', 'What happens now?', and 'why do I do that?', until a reasonable game of Snakes and Ladders is under way. Clearly, for the children to succeed, they must first be familiar with the game themselves.

Examples

Child says, 'You put it on there.' Teacher asks, 'Put what on where?' Child says, 'Your counter on there.' Teacher: 'Where is there?' Child: 'On the start. Now you throw the die'. (Teacher does so.) Teacher: 'What happens now?', and so on.

Tip

Try to avoid letting the children resort to pointing.

Extension

Try this with other games, for example Ludo.

Stage I
Stage II
Stage III
Stage IV
Circle Time
Hall/PE
Literacy
Numeracy
Drama
Small Group
Art
Humanities
Science

EXPLAINING

Finders Keepers

Aim
To be able to give instructions without using gesture.

Equipment

A bunch of keys to hide.

How to Play

Tell the children about Bizzo and Wacko (whom they may already have encountered!). These two characters share a home, and Bizzo is always losing the keys. Choose two children to act the parts of Bizzo and Wacko. Remind the rest of the group that they must try to be very quiet while Wacko tells Bizzo where to look. The child playing the part of Bizzo goes outside the room, while Wacko hides the keys. Wacko then tells him to come back in. When Bizzo comes in he must stand still until Wacko tells him what to do. Wacko must then give instructions, one at a time, to lead Bizzo to the hidden keys. If possible, demonstrate the activity first with another adult, emphasising that they must not give the exact location straight away.

Example

'Go to the window, look on the shelf, find the big red book, look behind it.'

EXPLAINING

	Stage I
	Stage II
	Stage III
	Stage IV

Tracks

| | Circle Time |

Aim

To be able to explain the course of footprints drawn on a simple pictorial map.

| | Hall/PE |

Equipment

'Tracks' maps from Teaching Resources, half with tracks marked, half without.
The marked maps show footprints going from a starting point to a finishing point.

| | **Literacy** |

How to Play

Photocopy sets of marked and unmarked maps. Divide the children into pairs. One child in each pair (Child A) has a map with the tracks marked on it, the other child (Child B) has a matching map, but without the tracks. Explain that the children with the marked maps have to tell their partner where the tracks go, step by step. Child B attempts to draw the course of the footprints as explained, on his map. At the end, the two compare their maps.

	Numeracy
	Drama
	Small Group

Examples

A snow scene with bird footprints going from a Christmas tree to a barn, from the barn to a pond, around the pond, behind a house, through a gate and up on to a bird-table.
A desert island with human footprints going from the edge of the sea, around some rocks, across a stream, up a hill, to find a treasure chest.

	Art
	Humanities
	Science

Tips

Before playing this game, you may need to take one child as your partner and act as the instructor, while the rest of the group look on. It is a simple game, but quite difficult to explain.

Speaking, Listening & Understanding
USING SPOKEN LANGUAGE

NARRATING

Stage I

Stage II

Stage III

Stage IV

Circle Time

Hall/PE

Literacy

Numeracy

Drama

Small Group

Art

Humanities

Science

NARRATING

Picture Stories

Aim
To be able to tell a story from a picture sequence.

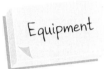
Equipment

Sequential story pictures, cut into individual cards. (Several sets of sequencing pictures are available commercially. These range from easy two- or three-picture sequences to more complex ones, eg, ColorCards®.)

Preparation

Choose a picture sequence. Photocopy and cut up the pictures into individual cards.

How to Play

Divide the children into pairs. Hand the first picture in the sequence to the first pair of children. They must come to the front of the group and say what happened in their picture. The next picture in the sequence is given to another pair, who again come out and relate the event shown in their picture. Continue in this way until the story is complete.

Tip

When prompts are needed, encourage the children to relate the story in the past tense by saying 'What happened next? Then what happened?'

NARRATING

Stage I

Stage II

Stage III

Stage IV

Circle Time

Hall/PE

Literacy

Numeracy

Drama

Small Group

Art

Humanities

Science

Once Upon a Time (1)

Aim
To be able to order a picture story into the correct sequence, and relate the story.

Equipment

Sequential pictures stories. (Several sets of sequencing pictures are available commercially. These range from easy two- or three-picture sequences to more complex ones, eg, ColorCards®.)

Preparation

Copy enough complete picture stories for half the number of children playing. Then copy matching sets, which will be cut up into individual picture cards.

How to Play

Divide the children into pairs, seated opposite each other with a screen between them. Give one of each pair a complete picture story sheet, which has the pictures in the correct sequence. Give the second member of the pair the corresponding individual pictures jumbled up in any order, spread out in front of them. The child with the complete story tells it slowly, one picture at a time, giving the other child time to find the right picture and arrange it in order.

Tip

You can let the pairs work one at a time so that the others can listen, or separate the pairs widely enough for them to be able to play simultaneously.

Stage I

Stage II

Stage III

Stage IV

Circle Time

Hall/PE

Literacy

Numeracy

Drama

Small Group

Art

Humanities

Science

NARRATING

Scrambled Stories

Aim
To be able to sequence and relate events in the right order.

Sequential pictures stories. (Several sets of sequencing pictures are available commercially. These range from easy two- or three-picture sequences to more complex ones, eg, ColorCards®.)

Choose one of the picture stories, photocopy it and cut it up into individual pictures.

This game is best played with a fairly small group of not more than six or so. Give each child a noise-maker (a drum, triangle or whistle). Tell the children the simple story you have chosen, showing each picture as you go, and putting them out in order in front of the children. Then pick up the pictures, shuffle them, and lay them out in front of the children all muddled up. Start to re-tell the story according to the pictures. Whenever the children spot a mistake in the proper sequence they must bang their drum, blow their whistle, or beat their triangle. One child (perhaps the first to play his instrument) is then given the opportunity to say what should have been the next event. The teacher corrects his 'mistake', and replaces the wrong picture with the right one. Continue in this way until the story has been 'unscrambled' to the end.

You may need to make the mistakes in the sequence extremely obvious at first.

NARRATING

Stage I

Stage II

Stage III

Stage IV

Circle Time

Hall/PE

Literacy

Numeracy

Drama

Small Group

Art

Humanities

Science

Shaggy Dog Story

Aim
To be able to make up a plausible story.

Equipment

None.

How to Play

Sit the children in a circle. Explain that together you are going to make up a story. If possible, ask another adult to write down the story as it evolves. Choose a child to start the activity, if necessary prompting for a suitable initial sentence. The next child repeats what the first child said, and adds an item of his own. Continue in this way, repeating the previous items, and adding a new one, until everyone has had a turn. At the end, read back the whole version. Discussion can then take place on how plausible the story is, and whether any changes need to be made.

Example

'Once upon a time… there was a frog… and he lived in a deep pond. One day in the summer…', and so on.

Tips

The children will probably need quite a lot of help at first. Tell them when a sentence is long enough, and encourage them to start new sentences. The person scribing only needs to write down the new additions to the story. Alternatively, use a tape recorder.

Extension

This activity could be incorporated into Sentence and Word Level work in the Literacy Hour.

Stage I

Stage II

Stage III

Stage IV

Circle Time

Hall/PE

Literacy

Numeracy

Drama

Small Group

Art

Humanities

Science

NARRATING

We Know the Story

Aim

To be able to retell a familiar story without visual prompts.

Equipment

None.

How to Play

Choose a story with which the children are familiar. Give them a brief outline of the story. Ask the children for 'hands up' to retell bits of the story one at a time until it is completed. Each contribution is written on a piece of paper and handed to the child who gave the information. When they get to the end of the story, collect all the written contributions. Read them out, one at a time. If they are not in the right order, help the children reorder them.

NARRATING

Stage I

Stage II

Stage III

Stage IV

Circle Time

Hall/PE

Literacy

Numeracy

Drama

Small Group

Art

Humanities

Science

Watch Me!

Aim
To be able to relate a sequence of actions.

None, or a few pieces of PE apparatus. A watch with a second-hand does help.

This game is best played in the hall. Divide the children into two teams, A and B. Choose one child from Team A, and tell him he has 30 seconds in which to do as many things of his own choice as he can manage, while everyone else watches. Now choose a child from Team B to relate the actions. If something is missed out, or in the wrong order, anyone can chip in a correction. Then repeat, choosing a child from Team B to carry out a series of actions, and a child from Team A to be the narrator.

Do a somersault on the mat; balance along the bench; touch the wallbars; look out of the window, and sit down.

Speechmark *Speaking, Listening & Understanding* PAGE 137
© C Delamain & J Spring 2003

Stage I

Stage II

Stage III

Stage IV

Circle Time

Hall/PE

Literacy

Numeracy

Drama

Small Group

Art

Humanities

Science

NARRATING

Time to Mime (1)

Aim
To be able to relate a series of actions.

Equipment

A few simple props such as a hat, an umbrella, a book, a pair of glasses, or a handbag.

How to Play

This game needs two adults at first, though later the children may be able to take over one or both of the acting roles. One adult leaves the room. The other comes in and performs a short mime. (For example, she sits down; looks at a book, mimes being unable to see clearly; then rummages in her bag for glasses; puts them on, and mimes relief at now being able to see to read.) The second adult comes in. The children give her the props, and then 'coach' her in her role, until she has repeated the sequence of actions carried out by her colleague.

Examples

1 Teacher comes in, takes off hat and coat, yawns and stretches, sits down, lifts imaginary cat on to lap, strokes it, and falls asleep.

2 Teacher comes to imaginary door, looks out, holds out hand to feel the rain, shakes head in disgust, goes inside again, turns on the TV, and sits down.

Tip

A certain amount of calling out and disagreement should be allowed in this game, and the second actor can ask for clarification if necessary. ('What did I do wrong?'; 'What should I have done?; 'What do I do next?') At the end, the teacher may want to draw attention to things that were left out or incorrect.

Speechmark ⓟ This page may be photocopied for instructional use only. *Speaking, Listening & Understanding*

NARRATING

Stage I

Stage II

Stage III

Stage IV

Circle Time

Hall/PE

Literacy

Numeracy

Drama

Small Group

Art

Humanities

Science

Second Half

Aim
To be able to complete complex sentences.

Equipment

Word and sentence list from Teaching Resources.

How to Play

Divide the children into teams or groups. Start with one team. Tell them that they are going to help you finish off some sentences, and you are going to see how many sentences you can complete between you in a given time (say two minutes). Then start off with the first incomplete sentence, and ask the first child in the team to complete it. Move quickly on to the next sentence and the next child, and so on.
Keep a tally of the number of sentences, and then see how well the second team can do.

Examples

'When I was a baby, I …'
'If we could fly, we …'

Tip

You may need a strategy to ensure that any child who cannot cope with this activity is not made to feel inadequate. You might pair such a child with a more able one, or allow the child to make marks on the board to keep the score.

Stage I

Stage II

Stage III

Stage IV

Circle Time

Hall/PE

Literacy

Numeracy

Drama

Small Group

Art

Humanities

Science

NARRATING

Once Upon a Time (2)

Aim
To be able to order the sequence of a set of pictures, and relate the story.

Commercial sets of sequential pictures (for example, ColorCards®).

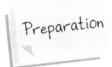

Choose one or more of the picture stories. Make sets of individual cards by copying the picture story sheets and cutting them up. You will need enough sets of individual cards for half the class.

Divide the children into pairs. Give each pair one of the sets of pictures, jumbled up in any order, spread out in front of them. Tell them that they are to work together to try to arrange the pictures to tell a story. The first to finish tells the story to the rest of the class.

This activity may lead to considerable discussion.

NARRATING

Stage I

Stage II

Stage III

Stage IV

Tall Story

Aim
To be able to create a simple narrative.

Circle Time

Equipment

None.

Hall/PE

How to Play

The children should be seated in a semicircle facing you. The aim of the game is to embellish a very basic opening sentence to form a simple narrative. If two adults are available, it will be easier to model it to the group. Start with the basic sentence – for example, 'John was in the garden.' The other adult embellishes the sentence and/or adds another. 'John was in the garden digging. Suddenly he heard a noise.' The first adult continues, 'Suddenly he heard a noise coming from behind a tree.' You may need to give the children a lot of help initially, but once they have got the idea, they enjoy the challenge of adding more and more preposterous or exciting parts to the story.

Literacy

Numeracy

Drama

Small Group

Art

Tip

Try taping the story as it develops.

Humanities

Extension

Children could write parts of the story during the Literacy Hour.

Science

Stage I

Stage II

Stage III

Stage IV

Circle Time

Hall/PE

Literacy

Numeracy

Drama

Small Group

Art

Humanities

Science

NARRATING

I've Been There

Aim
To be able to tell others about an outing.

Equipment

None.

How to Play

Go round the class or group, asking each child to think of an outing they have been on. This may range from a trip to Disneyland in America, to a visit to the local park and playground. All expeditions are equally valid. Then choose a child to tell the others as many things as they possibly can about their outing. Stipulate that they must produce a minimum of five facts or ideas in the time allotted. Two minutes is about right. Each narrator is rewarded with a round of applause.

Tip

Prompting may be required. Some ideas: 'How did you get there?', 'Who did you go with?', ' When did this happen?', 'How long did it all take?', 'Where did you stay?', 'What did you play on?'

Extension

You can turn this into a team or individual contest by making the person or team who produces the most ideas the winner.

NARRATING

Postcards

Stage I

Stage II

Stage III

Stage IV

Circle Time

Hall/PE

Literacy

Numeracy

Drama

Small Group

Art

Humanities

Science

Aim
To be able to give a short account of a holiday.

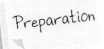

Pictures of different holiday destinations, preferably old postcards.

Make a list on the whiteboard of various different holiday destinations – for example, seaside, mountains, pony trekking, walking, farm, camping, theme park.

The children are going to choose a holiday card, and describe the picture to the rest of the group without showing them the card. The group will then decide what sort of holiday it is, and a tally mark will be made against that kind of holiday on the whiteboard. Each child takes a turn, and marks are awarded for complete sentences, interesting adjectives, and any other criteria that are appropriate at the time.

Give a demonstration first, and draw the children's attention to the use of good sentences, interesting adjectives, etc.

Writing the postcards could be an activity in the Literacy Hour.

Stage I

Stage II

Stage III

Stage IV

Circle Time

Hall/PE

Literacy

Numeracy

Drama

Small Group

Art

Humanities

Science

NARRATING

Time to Mime (2)

Aim
To be able to relate a series of actions, with visual prompts.

Equipment

A few simple props for each 'scenario', such as a handbag and contents.

How to Play

Divide the children into two or more teams or small groups. Teacher pretends to leave the room, and returns to perform a short mime. (For example, they sit down; take out a powder compact; look in a mirror, and pretend to powder their nose; take out a comb and pretend to comb their hair; replace compact and comb, and close bag.)

The teacher then lays out the props in front of the children, who are asked to retell the sequence of the mime. Children are picked in turn from the various groups. Teacher should prompt and encourage by holding up the various props if necessary, and by questioning ('What did I do first?'; 'What happened after that?'; 'What next?'; 'Is that in the right order?')

Extension

Make the scenarios longer.
See if the children can retell the whole scenario against the clock (eg, one minute).

NARRATING

Hatch a Plot

Aim
To be able to invent and relate a coherent story using some basic ideas.

Assorted sets of pictures from Teaching Resources.

Divide the children into small groups (about four or five to a group).The groups can choose their picture set. They are then given five minutes to invent a story around the pictures they have chosen. One child from each group narrates their story to the rest of the class.

A typical picture set includes a zebra, a bucket, a man, a car and a boy.

Once the children have got the idea, you could make this into a more exciting activity by encouraging the audience to clap after each story is told, and timing the length of the applause. The group earning the longest applause is the winning group.

Stage I

Stage II

Stage III

Stage IV

Circle Time

Hall/PE

Literacy

Numeracy

Drama

Small Group

Art

Humanities

Science

Stage I
Stage II
Stage III
Stage IV
Circle Time
Hall/PE
Literacy
Numeracy
Drama
Small Group
Art
Humanities
Science

NARRATING

What a Star!

Aim
To be able to think up and relate everyday activities.

Equipment

None.

How to Play

Tell the children that this game is about a boy called Buster. (If your class or group consists of more girls than boys, this can simply be changed to a girl called Betsy.) This child is exceptionally good, well-behaved and kind. He was so good one day that he did 10 good things and won a medal. Can the children think of 10 good things he might have done? Go round the group in turn.

Examples

Helped with the washing up.
Fed the hamster.
Tidied the school book tray.

Extension

This activity can lead in to a discussion about what good things the children themselves may have done, which things are hardest, and why.
The game could also be played thinking up naughty things, or with one group thinking of good things and the other group naughty things.

NARRATING

Stage I

Stage II

Stage III

Stage IV

Circle Time

Hall/PE

Literacy

Numeracy

Drama

Small Group

Art

Humanities

Science

How Can You Tell?

Aim
To be able to think of and relate reasons for an imagined situation.

Equipment

None.

How to Play

This game is best played with not more than about 10 children, seated in a circle around you. Explain that you are going to tell them about some strange happenings. The children are to think up the possible reasons for becoming aware of these happenings. Keep going around the circle asking for ideas, until the supply runs dry. Then move on to the next 'happening'.

Examples

How can you tell...that there is a monster in the cellar?
How can you tell...that there has been a mouse in the kitchen?
How can you tell...that a bird is trapped in the attic?
How can you tell...that there was a big party in the house last night?

Speaking, Listening & Understanding
USING SPOKEN LANGUAGE

PREDICTING

PREDICTING

Stage I
Stage II
Stage III
Stage IV
Circle Time
Hall/PE
Literacy
Numeracy
Drama
Small Group
Art
Humanities
Science

What If?

Aim

To be able to predict what will happen next.

Equipment

None.

Preparation

Make a list of situations, as described in the examples below. Make sure there is at least one situation for each member of the group.

How to Play

Read a situation to each child in turn. The child has to tell the rest of the group what he thinks might happen next. Repeat what he has said to the rest of the group, and ask their opinion. If they agree, move on to the next child.

Examples

'What will happen if…'

I mix red and yellow paint?

I put a heavy brick in the pond?

I leave the toast in the toaster?

I keep driving my car when the petrol gauge says empty?

I wear a short-sleeved shirt in the winter?

I leave my purse in the supermarket?

I put a paper clip near a magnet?

I put a rubber near a magnet?

Tip

The situations can reflect work in Science or Humanities.

PREDICTING

Stage I

Stage II

Stage III

Stage IV

Circle Time

Hall/PE

Literacy

Numeracy

Drama

Small Group

Art

Humanities

Science

Cargoes

Aim
To make a verbal prediction.

Equipment

A paper boat for each member of the group.
A large container of water – the bigger the better.

Preparation

Make the paper boats – this could be done by the children, but they will probably need quite a lot of help. Collect some small items which will be the 'cargo' – paperclips, cotton wool, screwed up tissue paper, rubbers, small cubes, etc. These should be arranged in separate piles (one for each member of the group, or each pair if they are working in pairs).

How to Play

Each child or pair chooses a cargo, and carefully loads their boat. When everyone is ready, they take turns to explain how they think their boat will fare when it has to go to sea with its cargo. Write down each prediction, then let the children take turns to launch their boat, and see if their prediction was right.

Extension

Discussion can follow about why some boats were more successful than others. Results could be recorded in a variety of ways, including graphs and pie charts. If you have a river or a stream, why not have a boat race?

Stage I

Stage II

Stage III

Stage IV

Circle Time

Hall/PE

Literacy

Numeracy

Drama

Small Group

Art

Humanities

Science

PREDICTING

Chain Reaction

Aim
To be able to predict the next part of a sequence of events.

Equipment

None.

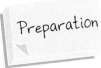

Preparation

Make a list of situations that could give rise to a chain of events – see examples below. Write them on small pieces of paper, fold them, and put them in a container.

How to Play

Everyone sits on chairs in a circle. The first child takes a piece of paper from the container, and is helped to read what it says. The child next to him has to say what happens next, as an outcome of the first event. Carry on taking turns around the circle, to add further events. These can be as preposterous as you like, but each addition must be a plausible consequence of the preceding event.

Examples

Mr Jones overslept – he dressed in a hurry and put on odd socks.
Emma stubbed her toe so hard that she punched her brother.
Ryan missed the bus, so he had to walk to school.
Katie found a £2 coin.

Speechmark ⓟ This page may be photocopied for instructional use only. *Speaking, Listening & Understanding*
© C Delamain & J Spring 2003

PREDICTING

Stage I

Stage II

Stage III

Stage IV

Circle Time

Hall/PE

Literacy

Numeracy

Drama

Small Group

Art

Humanities

Science

Story Switch

Aim
To be able to predict what will happen next.

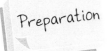

None.

Choose some stories that are familiar to the children. These could be well-known fairy stories, or stories that they have recently heard – for example, in Literacy Hour. Alter an important part of the plot, and write a list of the alterations you have made. See examples below.

Tell the children that some of the stories they know well have been changed. Each child has a turn at trying to tell the rest of the group what happens after the changed part of the story. Their responses could be written down, or recorded on an audio tape. Alternatively, the same story could be presented to the whole group, and everyone draws a picture of what happened next. When the drawings are finished, each child tells his ending.

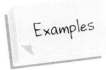

Goldilocks didn't go to sleep in Baby Bear's bed. Instead, she hid in a cupboard.
Cinderella danced with the prince, but secretly she didn't like him at all.
The giant chased Jack down the beanstalk, and managed to land safely on the ground.

Stage I

Stage II

Stage III

Stage IV

Circle Time

Hall/PE

Literacy

Numeracy

Drama

Small Group

Art

Humanities

Science

PREDICTING

Banana Skins!

Aim
To be able to verbally predict the consequence of an action.

Equipment

The 'Wacko's Wand' template from Teaching Resources.

Preparation

You will need several different copies of the picture. On each picture you will need to draw an additional item (see examples below).

How to Play

Show the children the main picture (without any additions), and explain that this is Wacko the Wizard's kitchen. They may already be familiar with the wizard from activities in the sections on Inference and Describing. Then select one of the pictures to which you have added a drawing. Tell the children that Wacko's friend, Bizzo the alien, sometimes comes into the kitchen when Wacko isn't there and meddles with things. Show them the picture you have selected, and ask them what will happen when Wacko comes back.

Examples

A banana skin in the doorway.
The sink full and the tap still running.
A frog behind one of the cushions on the sofa.
The window open and a storm outside.
An egg on the floor just inside the door.
A magic rug that makes you disappear on the floor by the table.

PREDICTING

Stage I

Stage II

Stage III

Stage IV

Circle Time

Hall/PE

Literacy

Numeracy

Drama

Small Group

Art

Humanities

Science

Prediction Pairs

Aim

To be able to match two parts of a statement to make a plausible prediction.

Equipment

'Prediction Pairs' template from Teaching Resources.

Preparation

Make a copy of the template, on to card if you want it to be durable. Cut along the dotted lines, so that the statements are in two separate parts. On the back of the sentence-start cards put a dot in one colour. On the back of the 'sentence-ending' cards put a different coloured dot.

How to Play

Lay all the cards face down on the table. Half will be one colour, and the other half, the other colour. Now proceed as for any game of pairs. The first child picks up a card of each colour. Help him to read what each card says. If this makes a plausible prediction, he may keep the pair. Continue until all the pairs have been claimed. The one with the most is the winner.

Extension

You can always add further prediction statements to the collection. Make sure that there is only one correct and plausible combination, otherwise it will get very confusing!

Stage I

Stage II

Stage III

Stage IV

Circle Time

Hall/PE

Literacy

Numeracy

Drama

Small Group

Art

Humanities

Science

PREDICTING

Look Out!

Aim
To be able to imagine future events and express the ideas.

Equipment

Situations from Teaching Resources.

How to Play

Explain to the children that you are going to start off some little stories, but you can never remember quite what happens. When you get stuck, you will ask the children to put their hands up if they think they know what will happen next. Encourage discussion based on the suggestions, and perhaps elicit a train of consequences. Note that the stories must be told in the *present tense.* Embellish them as much as you care to!

Examples

Someone has let go of a balloon, and it is floating towards a very prickly holly tree. Challenge the children to come up with two alternative predictions. Take suggestions in turn.

Tip

When asking for suggestions, use either 'What do you think *will* happen?', or 'What *might* happen?'

PREDICTING

Stage I

Stage II

Stage III

Stage IV

Circle Time

Hall/PE

Literacy

Numeracy

Drama

Small Group

Art

Humanities

Science

Poor Mr Pig

Aim
To be able to make predictions on the basis of probability.

Equipment

Stories from Teaching Resources.
Counters for each child.

How to Play

Explain to the children that you are going to read them a story. It is about Mr Pig, who is very, very big and fat. While they listen to the story, they must try to spot situations in which they think Mr Pig would probably have got into dreadful difficulties. Every time they think they have spotted one, they must put out one of their counters. At the end, you will see who has got nearest to the right number. Then you will read the story again and tell them what *really* happened, with all the disasters included.

Example

Mr Pig looked out of his window and saw that it was a lovely sunny day. He badly wanted to go to the beach, but his car was being mended. 'Never mind', he thought, 'I'll take Mrs Pig's little minicar, she won't need it today.' He packed a big picnic basket, and climbed into the car. (*Got stuck.*) Off down the road he went. When he reached the seaside, he popped into a shop to buy a sun-hat and some sun-cream. He went in through the revolving doors (*got stuck again*) and up in the lift, which was very small. (*Stuck once more.*) When he had finished his shopping, he waddled down to the beach, and lowered himself into a deckchair. (*Chair broke.*)

Stage I

Stage II

Stage III

Stage IV

Circle Time

Hall/PE

Literacy

Numeracy

Drama

Small Group

Art

Humanities

Science

PREDICTING

Oh Dear!

Aim
To be able to predict an outcome based on general knowledge.

Equipment

None.

How to Play

Tell the children that some friends of yours are planning a day out at the seaside. They will be taking a sun umbrella, sun-hats, a rug, a picnic, swimming costumes, a lilo for floating on, and books to read. If possible, sketch these things roughly on a board or whiteboard. Before setting out, the family rings up the resort to find out what conditions are going to be like. Pass on the information to the children, and ask for ideas as to what this will mean for your friends' day out. How many can they think of?

Examples

There is going to be a very, very strong wind all day. (The umbrella will blow away, sand will blow into the picnic, the lilo might blow out to sea, hats blow away, etc.)
It is going to be unusually hot.
A lot of tar is coming in on the tide towards the beach.
It is going to be extremely cold.
It is likely to rain.

Tip

Encourage the children to pursue their ideas, by saying 'So?', 'And then?', 'And what next?'

PREDICTING

Stage I

Stage II

Stage III

Stage IV

Circle Time

Hall/PE

Literacy

Numeracy

Drama

Small Group

Art

Humanities

Science

What Would They Say?

Aim

To be able to predict what two characters might say to one another.

Equipment

None.

Preparation

Make a list of well-known story, nursery-rhyme or TV characters, and write them on cards.

How to Play

Go through the cards with the children, making sure everyone is familiar with all the chosen characters. If there are any unfamiliar ones, they need to be rejected. Now shuffle the cards. Two children are then asked to take a card from the pile. Help them read who the characters are. They then have to try to think of something appropriate to say to the other character, based on what they know about that character. Once everyone is familiar with the activity, you can make it more of a game by letting one child be the caller. He calls the names of two children in the group, and they take a card each. At the end of their turn, they each call another child, and that pair take a card each.

Examples

Bob the Builder	Barbie	Bart Simpson
Humpty Dumpty	Cinderella	Buffy the Vampire Slayer
Harry Potter	Rugrats	Red Riding Hood
The Lion King	Postman Pat	

Extension

Children could then write what the characters said, using prepared speech bubbles.

Stage I

Stage II

Stage III

Stage IV

Circle Time

Hall/PE

Literacy

Numeracy

Drama

Small Group

Art

Humanities

Science

PREDICTING

Magic Carpet

Aim
To be able to predict a consequence.

Equipment

None.

Preparation

The children in the group are going to own a magic carpet. You are going to find out that they have the carpet, and ask lots of questions about it. Make a list of the kind of questions you want to ask.

How to Play

Tell the group that they have somehow got hold of a carpet – not just any old carpet, but a *magic* one. They will need some time to think about this, and to discuss with each other where they got the carpet; who knows about it; where they can go on it, etc. Tell them that you have found out that they have this carpet, and you need to ask some questions. They then take turns to be in the hot seat. Ask each child a question, and record both question and answer.

Examples

'Where did you get the carpet?'; 'How many people can fit on it?'; 'Is it safe?'; 'How do you know it's magic?'; 'Are there any rules about who can go on it?'; 'Who else knows about it?'; 'What if you want to come down again?'; 'What if someone feels airsick?'; 'What if it lands in the sea?'; 'What if it lands on top of a mountain?'; 'How do you get back home again?'

PREDICTING

	Stage I
	Stage II
	Stage III
	Stage IV
	Circle Time
	Hall/PE
	Literacy
	Numeracy
	Drama
	Small Group
	Art
	Humanities
	Science

What Can We Do?

Aim
To be able to predict an appropriate action.

Equipment

'What Can We Do' scenarios from Teaching Resources.

How to Play

Explain to the children that they will need to do some pretending. Select a confident child to start the activity. Choose one of the scenarios and explain it to him. He then mimes the scenario, and how he feels about it. Tell the rest of the group the scenario, and ask what they should do to enable the desired outcome. The child who gives the best answer is chosen to act out the next scenario. The game can continue as long as you wish.

Extension

Compile a list of 'Why?' questions to match the scenarios. Then ask, for example, *'Why was Ben sad?'*

Stage I

Stage II

Stage III

Stage IV

Circle Time

Hall/PE

Literacy

Numeracy

Drama

Small Group

Art

Humanities

Science

PREDICTING

Raffle Prize

Aim
To be able to verbally predict what someone might choose.

Equipment

'Raffle Prize' texts from Teaching Resources.
Pictures from Teaching Resources.

Preparation

Cut out the 'Prize' pictures.

How to Play

Explain that you are going to tell them about some children who have each won a prize in a raffle. (You may have to explain what a raffle is.) You could use dollshouse or Lego® figures to represent the children. Set out the 'prizes' on a table, so that everyone can see them. Go through the prizes, making sure everyone knows what each one is. Then read out the first character description. No one is allowed to talk until you have read the description. When you have finished reading, ask which of the prizes that character will choose. Anyone who suggests an answer must be able to say why the character will choose that prize. Give the person who guesses the 'prize'. Continue with the next description, and so on, until all the prizes have been distributed. The winner is the child with the most prizes.

PREDICTING

Stage I

Stage II

Stage III

Stage IV

Circle Time

Hall/PE

Literacy

Numeracy

Drama

Small Group

Art

Humanities

Science

In Your Dreams

Aim

To be able to imagine a set of unusual circumstances, and explain what might happen.

Equipment

A bean-bag.

How to Play

Seat the children in a circle. Say you are going to tell them about some very odd dreams you have had. Then you are going to ask them what might happen if your dreams came true. The first child holds the bean-bag and thinks of a suggestion. He then passes the bean-bag on to the next child, who also tries to think up a possibility. The bean-bag continues around the circle until the children run out of ideas. Then a new 'dream' is begun.

Examples

It rains for a whole year. (Water comes up over the school. We have to go everywhere in boats; water comes into houses, and people have to live upstairs. There are ponds in everyone's garden, frogs take over the world, and we have to live in submarines.)
Everything is suddenly made of chocolate.
Christmas happens every week.
It's winter all year long.
There are no trees.
There are no cars, buses, trains or planes.
Animals can talk.
Pigs take over the world.
People live to be 200.
Everyone turns green overnight.

PREDICTING

Stage I

Stage II

Stage III

Stage IV

Circle Time

Hall/PE

Literacy

Numeracy

Drama

Small Group

Art

Humanities

Science

Hot Seat

Aim
To be able to make a verbal prediction.

Equipment

None.

Preparation

Choose a possible school trip. This could be fictitious, or even better, one that is really going to take place. Jot down the important details about the trip (see examples below). Make a list of 'What if?' questions relating to the trip.

How to Play

Tell the children that you are going to give them information about a school trip. If it is a fictitious trip, then you need to explain this quite clearly. Now read them the information about the trip. Next, explain that you are a teacher who worries about just about everything. They are all going to be in the 'hot seat' while you ask them questions. Ask the first question, and choose someone with their hand up to answer. Some of the answers might generate quite a lot of discussion. Keep asking different questions, aiming to allow each child to have a turn at making a prediction.

Examples

A school trip to the beach. Travelling by coach, taking packed lunch and swimming things. Allowed money for ice-cream. Must bring own sun-cream and a hat. *'What if's:* What if it rains? What if I forget my money? What if I get sick on a coach? What if I can't swim? What if I bring chocolate in my lunch box?

PREDICTING

Stage I

Stage II

Stage III

Stage IV

Circle Time

Hall/PE

Literacy

Numeracy

Drama

Small Group

Art

Humanities

Science

Soppy Bear and Smart Bear

Aim
To be able to predict actions based on knowledge of character.

Equipment

Two easily distinguishable teddies. (Or any other two toy animals or puppets who can be named Soppy and Smart.)

How to Play

Seat the children in a semicircle in front of you. Introduce the two bears (or other animals or puppets). Explain that Soppy Bear is a bit of a wimp. He cries a lot, and never knows what to do in tricky situations. Smart Bear, however, is sensible and confident, and nearly always takes appropriate action. Now throw one of the bears to a child, and explain the situation they find themselves in. (See examples.) 'What would he do?' When the child has answered, take the bear back, and throw one or other bear to the next child. Outline the next situation, and so on until everyone has had a turn.

Examples

His wellington boot is stuck in a grating.
He's fallen out of bed.
He's got lost in the supermarket.
He's dropped his school bag in a puddle.

Extension

Initiate a discussion about how we cope with this sort of problem. How could Soppy Bear be encouraged to be more grown-up? Do we know anyone like Soppy Bear?

PLAYING
WITH WORDS

Stage I

Stage II

Stage III

Stage IV

Circle Time

Hall/PE

Literacy

Numeracy

Drama

Small Group

Art

Humanities

Science

PLAYING WITH WORDS

Stamp and Jump

Aim
To be able to recognise the sound of the initial letter of your name.

Equipment

None.

How to Play

This is a rather noisy game, good for when the children need to let off steam.
Tell the children you are going to choose one sound at a time. You will call out 'If your name begins with…', and then you will tell them something to do. Several children may all be carrying out the action at the same time.

Examples

'If your name begins with ''ssss'' – stamp your foot.'
'If your name begins with ''mmm'' – turn round.'
'If your name begins with "ffff" – put your hand in the air.'

Extension

After some preliminary work on recognising the number of syllables in words, this game can be used in exactly the same way to reinforce syllable awareness. ('If your name has two syllables in it – shout out yes.')

Speechmark ⑤ Ⓟ This page may be photocopied for instructional use only. *Speaking, Listening & Understanding*

PLAYING WITH WORDS

Stage I

Stage II

Stage III

Stage IV

Circle Time

Hall/PE

Literacy

Numeracy

Drama

Small Group

Art

Humanities

Science

Syllable Hopscotch

Aim

To be able to match the right number of hops to the syllables in words.

Equipment

A notebook, and a biro or pencil to keep the score.

How to Play

This is a game for the hall or playground. Draw two 'hopscotch' grids on the floor, making the boxes big enough to hop or jump into comfortably. Divide the class into two teams, each team lined up at the end of one of the grids. Each team starts off with the same number of points. The first child from each team is now given a word. They can choose whether they will have a two-, three-, four- or five-syllable word. They then hop from box to box on their grid, saying the word broken up into syllables as they go (eg, ca-ter-pill-ar). If they step outside the box, put both feet down, or hop the wrong number of syllables, their team loses a point. If they do everything right, their team gains a point. The winning team is the one with the most points when everybody has had one or two turns.

Examples

rabbit, sausage, target, hamster, elbow (two syllables)
elephant, eiderdown, centipede, crocodile, dinosaur (three syllables)
alligator, binoculars, television, caterpillar, helicopter (four syllables)
communication, independently, educational, alphabetical (five syllables)

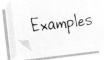

Stage I

Stage II

Stage III

Stage IV

Circle Time

Hall/PE

Literacy

Numeracy

Drama

Small Group

Art

Humanities

Science

PLAYING WITH WORDS

Post a Sound

Aim

To be able to recognise individual sounds in words.

Equipment

Three containers – for example, shoe boxes.

Preparation

You will need a collection of single-syllable pictures, which begin or end with your selected target sounds. (See examples below.)

How to Play

Set out the boxes so that they are clearly visible. Mark each with its target sound. Shuffle the pictures and place in a pile, face down. The first child takes the top picture, says what it is, then decides which box to put it in. He then has to say why it goes in that box – for example, because it has 'c' at the beginning, or because it ends with 's'. Carry on around the group until all the pictures have been 'posted'.

Examples

Target sounds: 'p', 's', 'ch'.
Pictures: pig, sun, chair, cup, bus, beach, peach, chip.

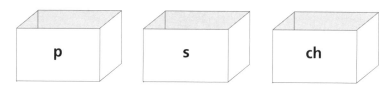

Tip

You will see that some of the pictures can be put into more than one box – the child can decide which one he wants it to be in.
Important: pronounce the sounds as a single unit, *do not* add a little 'uh' sound – 'puh', 'suh', 'chuh'.

PLAYING WITH WORDS

Stage I

Stage II

Stage III

Stage IV

Circle Time

Hall/PE

Word Sort

Literacy

Aim

To be able to sort words according to their initial sound.

Numeracy

Equipment

A selection of pictures starting with the target sounds: these could be cut out of catalogues, etc, or commercially produced pictures.

Drama

Preparation

Decide what target sounds you are going to choose (not more than three), and collect the relevant pictures.

Small Group

How to Play

Choose a child to represent each sound, and stand them in different parts of the room. Place the pictures face down on a table, and choose a child to take a picture. They must say what it is, then go to the correct 'sound' child. Continue in this way, taking turns to take a card and find its 'sound', until all the cards are used up.

Art

Examples

'c' – car, camera, cot, coat, carpet, key, kite.
'p' – pig, pot, pen, panda, pea, parrot, postman.
'm' – moon, man, mum, map, mug, meat.

Humanities

Extension

If the children find this really easy, extend the number of target sounds to four.

Science

Stage I

Stage II

Stage III

Stage IV

Circle Time

Hall/PE

Literacy

Numeracy

Drama

Small Group

Art

Humanities

Science

PLAYING WITH WORDS

Lucy's Luggage

Aim

To be able to recognise when words start with the same sound, and when they do not.

Equipment

None.

How to Play

Tell the children that you will give them a long list of things that Lucy is going to pack in her suitcase. She only wants things that begin with the same sound as her name. Whenever you say something that starts with a different sound, they are to call out 'Stop!'. Lucy will throw that item out of her suitcase. Keep going until you run out of ideas, and then introduce a different character with a different initial sound.

Examples

Lucy is taking a lamb, a lettuce, a *teddy bear,* some lollipops, a lorry, a loaf, a leaf, a *skirt,* a lamp, some lipstick, a locket, and a *book.*
Peter is taking some pills, some paper, some pepper, a *car,* a pipe, a poppy, some peas, some *chocolate,* and a pig.

Tip

Emphasise the sound as much as necessary to begin with.
It is a good idea to write the letter you are working on up on the board in both capital and lower case. Introduce it by its name as well as its sound.

Extension

See if the children can add to the list.

Speechmark ⑤ Ⓟ

PLAYING WITH WORDS

Your Rhyme

Aim
To be able to recognise if a word rhymes with your name.

Equipment

None, but you may want to jot down the rhyming words you have thought up for each child.

How to Play

Seat the children facing you. Tell them that you are going to call out some words, one at a time. Each one will rhyme with somebody in the group. It may rhyme with more than one! If a child thinks the word rhymes with his name, he must put his hand up, and if he is right, he gets a clap. If you are very quick-thinking, you can reward them with a little verse of their very own.

Examples

Josh/wash (Mum said Josh, have a wash.)
Jack/back (Dad called Jack, please come back.)

Tip

There will inevitably be some names in the class for which there is no rhyme. In this case, you might open a discussion, call for suggestions, and if the child is very disappointed, point out that it is more unusual *not* to have a rhyme than to have one!

Stage I	
Stage II	
Stage III	
Stage IV	
Circle Time	
Hall/PE	
Literacy	
Numeracy	
Drama	
Small Group	
Art	
Humanities	
Science	

Stage I

Stage II

Stage III

Stage IV

Circle Time

Hall/PE

Literacy

Numeracy

Drama

Small Group

Art

Humanities

Science

PLAYING WITH WORDS

Ridiculous Rhymes

Aim
To be able to think of a rhyming word for an unknown verse.

Equipment

'Ridiculous Rhymes' from Teaching Resources.

How to Play

Tell the children you are all poets, and you are going to make up some brand new rhyming verses. You will start them off, and see if they can help you to fill in the gaps. Read out your incomplete limerick, line by line. Do a bit of miming if the children are stuck. Listen to all suggestions for the missing words, and discuss which one would be best. Write the lines up on the board or flip-chart as the words are supplied, and then read the whole 'limerick' back to the class. Pause for them to call out the new words if they can.

Examples

A man had a very old car
He said 'This won't go very...' (far)

PLAYING WITH WORDS

Word Stew

Aim

To be able to judge whether words are in the same category.

Equipment

'Word Stew' cards from Teaching Resources.
A container for the cards.
A large hoop.

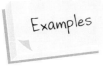

How to Play

The children sit on chairs in a circle with the hoop in the middle. Put the key word in the centre of the hoop, and the remaining words in the container. Read the key word to the children. Each child takes a card from the container. Read all the words as they are selected. When everyone has a card, say 'It's time to make the stew!' All the children with words in the key word category jump into the hoop.

Examples

Key word: rabbit
Words in container: cat, spoon, dog, mouse, crisps, horse, car.

Stage I
Stage II
Stage III
Stage IV
Circle Time
Hall/PE
Literacy
Numeracy
Drama
Small Group
Art
Humanities
Science

Stage I

Stage II

Stage III

Stage IV

Circle Time

Hall/PE

Literacy

Numeracy

Drama

Small Group

Art

Humanities

Science

PLAYING WITH WORDS

Rhyme Team

Aim
To be able to recognise rhyming words.

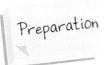

Equipment

Lists of rhyming words, see examples below.

Preparation

Make rhyming word cards from the lists below, or your own resources. There should be more than one pair for each rhyme family.

How to Play

Shuffle the cards. Divide the group into two teams. The teams should stand facing each other. Give each child a word card. They must be careful not to let the other team see their card. Choose a child to start the game. They must call out the names of two children in the opposite team. They hold their word cards up, and the chosen child must decide if the words rhyme. If they do, they score a point for their team. Now choose someone from the opposite team, and repeat the activity. You may like to put a time limit on this game – for instance, how many points can be scored in 10 minutes. By all means help the children read the words.

Examples

mat, bat, hat, cat, fat, rat
jug, mug, plug, bug, hug
lip, chip, ship, hip, rip, pip
bun, sun, gun, fun, one
man, van, fan, pan, can, ran
ball, wall, fall, hall, stall, tall

PLAYING WITH WORDS

Stage I

Stage II

Stage III

Stage IV

Opposites

Circle Time

Aim

To be able to match opposite pairs of words.

Hall/PE

Equipment

None.

Literacy

Preparation

Choose enough pairs of opposing words for each member of the group. Write the words in large print on sheets of A4 paper.

Numeracy

How to Play

Explain to the children that the aim of the game is to find their word 'partner'. You will need to make sure everyone knows the meaning of 'opposite' when referring to vocabulary. This might require a bit of practice before you start the game. Once you are sure all the children understand this, stick a word sheet to everyone's back. The idea is for them to find the person who has the opposite word on his back. This obviously involves reading, and there should be enough adults available to read the words for those who need it. When children have found their 'partner' they stand together.

Drama

Small Group

Art

Examples

Big/little, pretty/ugly, old/new, up/down, in/out, yes/no, easy/hard, black/white.

Humanities

Science

Extension

The words chosen could be linked to topic work as a means of reinforcing new vocabulary.

  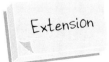

Stage I

Stage II

Stage III

Stage IV

Circle Time

Hall/PE

Literacy

Numeracy

Drama

Small Group

Art

Humanities

Science

PLAYING WITH WORDS

Catch a Word

Aim
To be able to think of a word beginning with a target sound.

A bean-bag.

The children stand in a circle. You start the game by throwing the bean-bag to one child, and saying a letter sound at the same time. That child must think of something that begins with that sound. If he is successful, he throws the bag to someone else, calling out a different letter sound. If he cannot think of a word, you may need to help. One way to do this is to give them some clues – for example 'something you can eat', or 'a pet animal'. Continue playing until everyone has had a turn.

The children may need some help thinking of different letter sounds at first – you could write familiar ones in large letters to remind them.

Speechmark

PLAYING WITH WORDS

Stage I
Stage II
Stage III
Stage IV
Circle Time
Hall/PE
Literacy
Numeracy
Drama
Small Group
Art
Humanities
Science

Peapods and Marshmallows

Aim

To be able to recognise the initial letter sound being used in a sentence, and find another word starting with the same sound.

Equipment

None.

How to Play

Explain to the children that you are going to give them special identities, and pretend that they are going shopping. They only buy things that start with the initial sound in their assumed name. Choose the first child, and give him his 'character'. Then read them their list of shopping choices slowly. Can they guess what they would buy? When they hear the right one, they call out 'Stop!' Give all the children a turn. At the end, see if each child can remember what his character was, and what he bought.

Examples

'Peter Piper packs a parcel with…'(mushrooms, lemon, peapods).

'Mickey Mouse munches…' (sausages, marshmallows, lemons, apples).

Additional characters: Boy Blue, Simple Simon, King Cole, Lucy Locket, Roland Rat, Adam Ant, Daring Dan. More characters can be gleaned from nursery rhymes, stories, films and reading schemes and, where necessary, invented.

Tip

Until the children are familiar with this sort of activity, emphasise the initial sounds as you say the words. If a child misses his item, go on to the end of the list and then repeat. The activity can be made harder by giving the children longer lists, and putting the target word towards the end.

Stage I

Stage II

Stage III

Stage IV

Circle Time

Hall/PE

Literacy

Numeracy

Drama

Small Group

Art

Humanities

Science

PLAYING WITH WORDS

Category Shopping

Aim
To be able to think of items belonging to specific categories.

Equipment

None.

How to Play

Choose two children to be the shoppers. Position them well apart from each other, in corners of the room. Group the rest of the children together. Tell the shoppers what category they are collecting, using the category name (eg, animals and food). Send them off, one at a time, to choose a child from the group. As they choose a child to take back to their corner, they must tell them what animal or food item they are. If you think their idea is seriously wrong, they must 'put' the child 'back on the shelf'. Which shopper can think up the most category items, and therefore collect the biggest group of children?

Examples

Animals, food, clothes, toys, transport/vehicles.

Tip

You can increase the number of shoppers if you have a large class or group.

Extension

Use narrower categories (farm animals, wild or zoo animals, fruit, vegetables).

Speechmark ⓟ This page may be photocopied for instructional use only. *Speaking, Listening & Understanding*
© C Delamain & J Spring 2003

PLAYING WITH WORDS

Stage I

Stage II

Stage III

Stage IV

Circle Time

Hall/PE

Literacy

Numeracy

Drama

Small Group

Art

Humanities

Science

Barbie® and Action Man®

Aim

To be able to recognise and think of words to suit a person or thing.

Equipment

None, but you may want to write yourself a list of words as memory joggers.

How to Play

Choose one child to be Barbie® and one to be Action Man®, and position them well apart from each other. The other children line up one behind the other. Tell them that you are going to call out lots of words. Some will best describe Barbie®, and some Action Man®. Starting with the first child in the line, call out a word and that child must go and stand beside either Barbie® or Action Man®. Call out another word, and the next child joins the appropriate group, and so on. Take it as fast as the children can manage. At the end, there will probably be some boys in the Barbie® group and some girls in the Action Man® group who may want to change. If they can think up a suitable word for the person whose group they wish to join, they can swap over. It doesn't matter if it is a word that has already been used.

Examples

Barbie®: pretty, dainty, beautiful, attractive, lovely, charming, sweet, gorgeous, fashionable, stylish.
Action Man®: big, strong, handsome, manly, brave, daring, hunky, smart, good-looking, powerful.

Extension

This game can be repeated with any sharply contrasting pairs of people, animals or objects.

Stage I

Stage II

Stage III

Stage IV

Circle Time

Hall/PE

Literacy

Numeracy

Drama

Small Group

Art

Humanities

Science

PLAYING WITH WORDS

Alphawords

Aim
To be able to generate words beginning with a target sound.

Equipment

None.

How to Play

The children sit in a circle. The letters of the alphabet should be displayed so that everyone can see them. Start the game by choosing the letter A, and saying a word that starts with 'a'. Encourage everyone in the group to think of different words that start with 'a'. Let the child next to you add the next word, and continue round the group, aiming to think of something beginning with 'a' for every member of the group. Then select the letter B, and repeat the process. Time restrictions will mean that you only ever use the first few letters, so vary it by letting children choose any letter. Write the words on a sheet of paper or the whiteboard.

Examples

A: ant, apple, and, Africa, add, anchor, Andrew, adder.

Tip

Some letters are obviously easier than others. Sometimes children will think up 'non-words' – these could be allowed, but listed on a separate sheet.

PLAYING WITH WORDS

Stage I

Stage II

Stage III

Stage IV

Tops and Tails

Circle Time

Aim

To be able to recognise final sounds and think of words with initial sounds.

Hall/PE

Literacy

Equipment

None.

How to Play

The children should sit in a circle. The idea is to think of a word that starts with the final sound of the word preceding it. This is not as complicated as it sounds! Start the activity by asking the child on your right to say a word. You may need to prompt him – for example, a piece of furniture, an animal, etc. You then take the final sound in that word and make up a new one beginning with that sound. The child on your left takes the final sound of your word, and generates one beginning with *that* sound. Continue round the group until everyone has had a turn.

Numeracy

Drama

Small Group

Art

Example

bed – dog – gate – ten – night – tall – lorry – even – nine – nice – sock – car – arm

Humanities

Science

Resources

TEACHING RESOURCES

Stage I

Following
Instructions

Jewellery Shop

Dotty

Stage III

Following Instructions

Stage III

Following
Instructions

Dotty (continued)

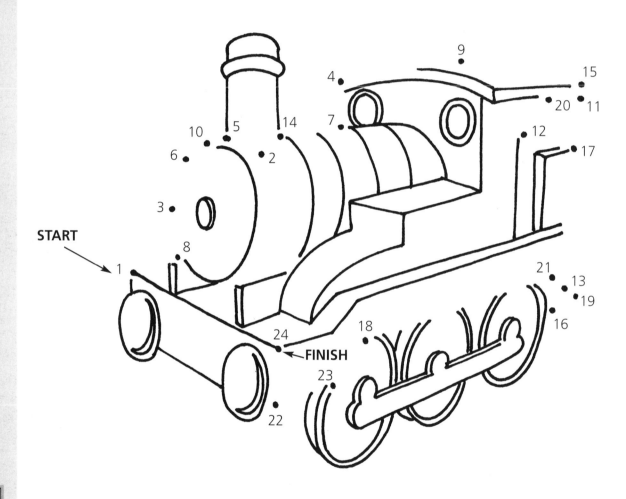

Speechmark **P** This page may be photocopied for instructional use only. *Speaking, Listening & Understanding*
© C Delamain & J Spring 2003

Dotty *(continued)*

Stage III

Following
Instructions

Stage IV

Following Instructions

Holiday Snaps

Seaside Pictures

1 The sun was shining. There were three little clouds in the sky. Far out at sea was a little red fishing boat with a blue sail. A boy and a girl were building a sandcastle on the beach. Near them, Mum lay sunbathing. Three little boys were paddling in the waves. A man stood on the rocks fishing.

2 Two boys were climbing on the rocks. A lady was walking her dog along the sand. There were three children swimming in the sea. A big ship was sailing across the horizon. The sun was partly hidden by a cloud. On the cliff there was a man walking.

3 Two children were playing in a rubber boat, in the waves. Their dad was paddling, holding the baby's hand. On the sand, a girl and boy had buried their mum – all you could see was her head and her toes. A speedboat was whizzing across the water. There were three seagulls flying in the sky.

Countryside Pictures

1 It was a sunny day. There was a red car parked by the gate into the field. A family were having a picnic – Mum, Dad and two boys. On the hill there were seven sheep grazing. There were lots of red poppies growing in the field. There was a big shady tree in the top corner of the field, where the two hedges joined.

2 Ben and Sam were flying their kite on the hill. It was sunny, but there were lots of clouds racing across the sky. In the field on the right, two horses munched grass. In the field on the left there were four cows. Yellow flowers grew beside the road. A bird sat on the gate-post.

3 There were three trees in the corner of the field. A rabbit was eating grass under the trees. At the bottom of the hill there was a little cottage. Smoke was coming out of the chimney. A lady was throwing sticks for her dog in the other field. It was a cloudy day, and it was starting to rain.

Speechmark Ⓟ This page may be photocopied for instructional use only. *Speaking, Listening & Understanding*

Holiday Snaps *(continued)*

Stage IV

Following Instructions

Holiday Snaps (*continued*)

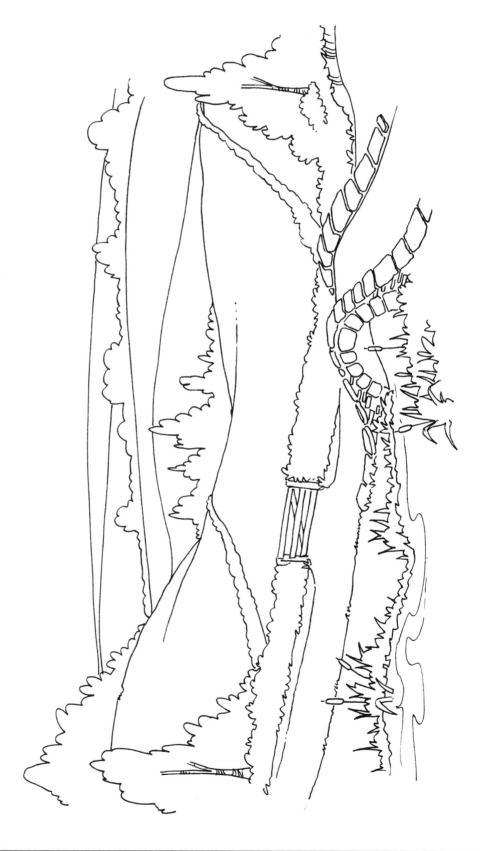

Amazing Mazes

Stage IV

Following
Instructions

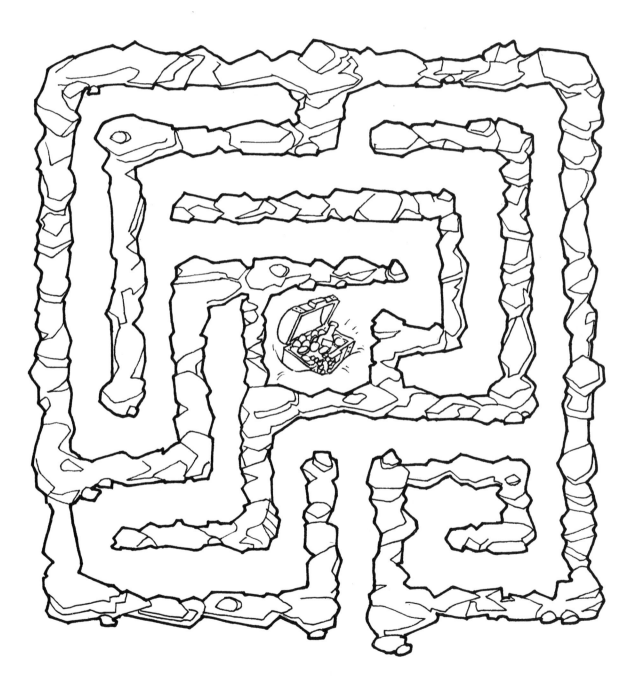

Stage IV

Following
Instructions

Amazing Mazes *(continued)*

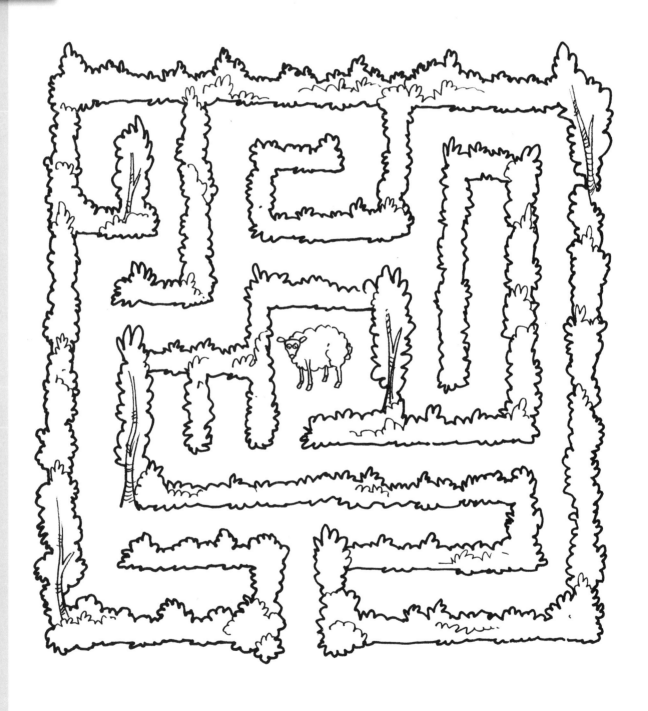

Bizzo's World

Stage I

Developing
Vocabulary

Stage I

Developing Vocabulary

Snakes and Ladders

You will need:
4 x '1 step forwards'
5 x '2 steps forwards'
5 x '3 steps forwards'
1 x '4 steps forwards'
6 x '1 step backwards'
5 x '2 steps backwards'
2 x '3 steps backwards'

1 step forwards

1 step backwards

2 steps forwards

2 steps backwards

3 steps forwards

3 steps backwards

4 steps forwards

Ready, Steady, Colour!

Shade in one of the shapes.

Fill in the apples on the tree.

Complete the gingerbread man.

Colour a piece of fruit.

Shade in a shape.

Fill in the snail's shell.

Complete the rhinoceros.

Colour another piece of fruit.

Shade in another shape.

Fill in the sail of the boat.

Complete the aeroplane.

Colour the other piece of fruit.

Marking the Sheets

Each child marks the sheet in front of them at the end of the activity. Tell the children to look at the drawings on the left – they should have a complete car, table and rabbit. Now look at the fruit – all the fruit should be coloured in. The shapes should all be shaded – that is, very lightly coloured. The heart, the apples and the sail should be coloured.

Stage III

Developing
Vocabulary

Ready, Steady, Colour! *(continued)*

Speechmark

More or Less Footsteps

Photocopy one number per child, and at least 10 extras to draw from. Copy the more/less than cards to equal the number of extra cards – these will be the packs you draw from.

0	1
2	3
4	5
6	7
8	9
more than	less than

Stage IV

Developing
Vocabulary

Leave One Out

Instructions:

Colour in all the shapes except the star.
Colour in all the shapes except the triangle.
Colour in all the shapes except the square.
Colour in all the shapes except the rectangle.
Colour in all the shapes except the circle.
Colour in all the shapes except the hexagon.
Colour in all the shapes except the star.
Colour in all the shapes except the triangle.
Colour in all the shapes except the square.
Colour in all the shapes except the circle.

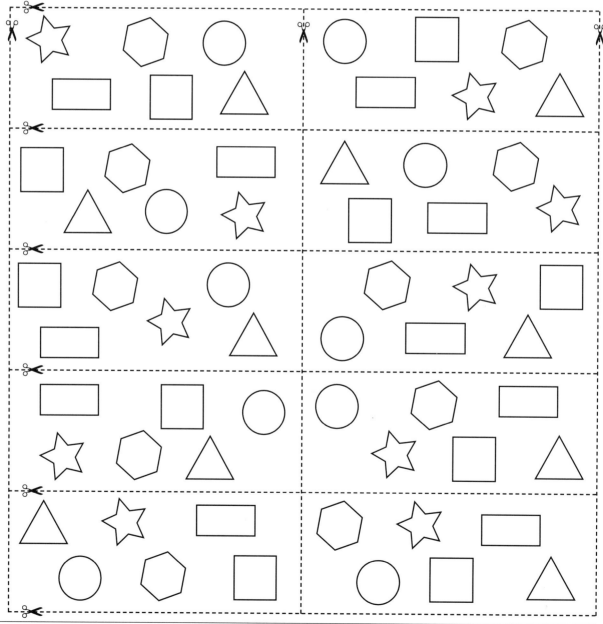

Speechmark ⑤ ℗ This page may be photocopied for instructional use only. *Speaking, Listening & Understanding*

Count Down

Instructions to the children

'You are going to put a dot on the shapes I tell you. Sometimes you won't have
to put any dots at all. We are going to start with the top box. Have you found
it? Put your finger on *all of the boxes*. Now get your crayons ready. Put a dot on
all of the boxes.'

'Now go down to the next box. Put a dot on *both of the circles*.'

'Now go down to the next box. Got the idea?'   'None of the triangles.'

Next box: 'Neither of the hexagons.'

Next box: 'Either of the rectangles.'

Next box: 'All of the stars.'

Next box: 'Either of the circles.'

Next box: 'Both of the triangles.'

Next box: 'Neither of the squares.'

Next box: 'None of the hexagons.'

Last box: 'All of the rectangles.'

Now tell the children to count their dots. They should have 16.

Stage IV

Developing
Vocabulary

Count Down (continued)

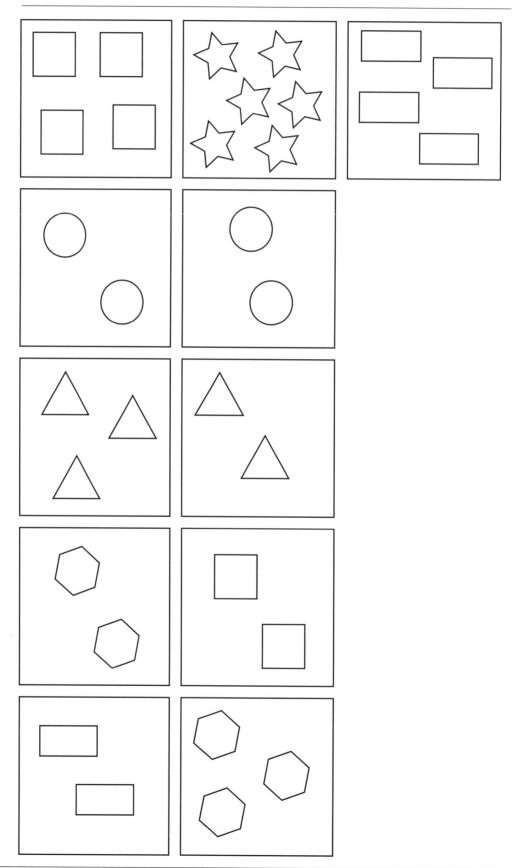

Story Spotter (1)

Stage I

Getting the
Main Idea

1 Last Saturday I went into town and bought a new sweater.

2 Sammy was a starfish who lived in a dark cave with his best friend.

3 If you don't clean your teeth and you eat lots of sweets, your teeth will go rotten.

4 If you go to the zoo you can see lots of interesting animals and reptiles.

5 My friend and I went to the beach for a picnic, but we got soaked because it started to rain.

6 It's really fun to support your favourite team at a football match.

7 My brother always gets the toy out of the cereal packet.

8 Cinderella was a girl who lived in a big house and had really unkind sisters, and she didn't have much fun.

Stage I

Getting the
Main Idea

Story Spotter (1)

1

2

3

4

5

6

7

8

Story Points (1)

Stage I

Getting the
Main Idea

The Princess

1   A long time ago a *beautiful princess* lived with her parents in a *castle*. Her name was Sarah and she had long blonde hair. Sarah was a lonely princess. (2 points)
2   One day she *was walking* in the gardens of the palace, beside the *lake,* when she heard someone calling 'Help me!'. She looked around, but she couldn't see anyone. (2 points)
3   Then she noticed something on the *island in the middle of the lake.* It was very small, about as big as your thumb. It was wearing bright *blue clothes,* and *riding on a dragonfly.* (3 points)
4   Sarah thought quickly. She picked up a long *piece of wood* and pushed it so that *one end touched the island and the other end touched the path.* (2 points)
5   The *tiny girl* climbed off the dragonfly and *walked carefully along the piece of wood.* When she reached the path, there was a p*uff of smoke.* (3 points)
6   The tiny creature had turned into *a normal sized girl* about the same age as Sarah. At last, *Sarah had a friend and* she stopped being lonely. (2 points)

TOTAL = 14 POINTS

Molly the Witch

1   There was once a *witch* called Molly who lived in a *red house*. She had a *cat* called Timmy. (4 points)
2   One day she went to the *shop. Timmy* followed her, carrying her magic *wand in his mouth.* (3 points)
3   *When she got to the shop*, she put some *apples* and a *bar of chocolate* in the *basket.* (4 points)
4   She opened her *bag* to get out her purse and realised she had left it at home. 'Oh no, what am I going to do?' she said to herself. Just then she saw *Timmy, with her wand.* (2 points)
5   She took the wand out of Timmy's mouth and *waved it,* and her *purse* appeared on the counter. (2 points)
6   Molly paid for her shopping, and bought a *large tin of salmon* for clever Timmy. (1 point)

TOTAL = 16 POINTS

Stage I

Getting the
Main Idea

Story Points (1) *(continued)*

Zoo Trip

1 There was once a *little girl* called Rosie. She had *plaits* and always wore *trousers.*(3 points)

2 One day she went to the *zoo* with *Nan and Grandad* and *her teddy*, who she always took everywhere. (3 points)

3 First they looked at the *giraffes*. There were *three* of them, in a big *field*. (3 points)

4 Then they went to the elephant pit. They *looked down* and saw a *mother elephant with her baby*. (3 points)

5 While Rosie was watching the baby elephant, she *dropped teddy* and he fell right down into the pit. Poor Rosie started to *cry*. (2 points)

6 Luckily the mother elephant was very clever. *She picked teddy up in her trunk* and *lifted it up high* so that *Grandad* could reach out and take it. (3 points)

TOTAL = 17 POINTS

The Scooter

1 This is a story about a *boy* called Ben. He had *black hair* and *wore glasses*. His best toy was his *scooter*. (4 points)

2 One Saturday *Ben* went out to the *shed* to get his scooter. But when he opened the door the *scooter had gone*! Someone had stolen it! (3 points)

3 Ben was *miserable*. No scooter, nothing to do. He *wandered round the garden*, *kicking the stones* on the path. (3 points)

4 Suddenly he heard a sound, coming from a tree. He *looked up* and saw a *bright green parrot*. (2 points)

5 The *parrot flew down* and *stood on the wall*. It looked at Ben and *said* "*Number 10, Castle Road*, Number 10, Castle Road'. (3 points)

6 Ben's friend Jamie lived at 10, Castle Road. *Ben went straight round there*, and discovered that Jamie had borrowed the scooter because his was broken. *Jamie* said sorry, and *Ben rode off on the scooter*. (3 points)

TOTAL = 18 POINTS

Story Points (1) *(continued)*

The Rock Pool

1 This story is about a *brother and sister* called Joe and Katie, who were on holiday at the *seaside*. (3 points)
2 It was a lovely *sunny* day and *they* went down to the *beach* with their *fishing nets and a bucket and spade each*. (7 points)
3 They found a big, deep *rock pool* and started *to fish*. Joe caught a *crab* and put it in his *bucket*. (4 points)
4 Katie didn't catch anything, and she was getting *fed up*, especially when Joe caught a *fish as well*. (2 points)
5 Just then something caught her eye, deep *down in the pool*. She very carefully dipped her *net in the water* and caught it. (2 points)
6 Katie had never seen anything so beautiful. There in her net was a *tiny mermaid*, with *long black hair* and *green scales on her fishy tail*. (3 points)

TOTAL = 21 POINTS

The Photo

1 This is another story about *Joe* and *Katie* on their seaside holiday. One afternoon they made a *huge sandcastle* on the beach and decorated it with *shells* and bits of *seaweed*. (5 points)
2 Then they dug a *moat* all the way round it, and let it fill up with *sea water*. Joe bought some flags from the shop, and they put *one* on the *top of the castle*. (4 points)
3 While they were building the castle, *Mum* and *Dad* were *leaning against the rocks*, sunbathing. Mum had her *sunglasses* on. Dad was reading a *book*. (5 points)
4 Dad said he wanted to take a photo of them standing by their castle. *Joe* and *Katie* stood one each side of the *castle*, smiling. *Bouncer*, their dog came and sat by Sam too. (4 points)
5 Dad was ages fiddling about with the camera. He held his *camera* up to his *eye* and told them to smile. Then he took a *step backwards*, not noticing the *rock pool* just behind him. (4 points)
6 He *fell into the pool* with a *splash*! Katie quickly grabbed the camera and *took a photo of him*. (3 points)

TOTAL = 25 POINTS

Stage I

Getting the
Main Idea

Titles (1)

1 THE BIRTHDAY PARTY – Mum was very busy all the morning. Jenni helped her stir the jelly, put little sugar stars on the cakes, and cut star-shaped biscuits with the special biscuit cutter. Then they blew up lots of balloons and hung them in bunches from the ceiling. Jenni was very excited. She couldn't wait for three o' clock to come.

2 THE STORM – Ben couldn't sleep. Although he was warm inside his sleeping bag, he was worried the tent might blow away. He could hear the wind roaring and the rain lashing the sides of the tent. Every few minutes there was a bright flash, and then the deafening sound of thunder.

3 LOST! – Old Mr Jones was digging his garden. It was a fine, sunny afternoon and there were lots of birds singing. He stopped for a rest and looked at the neat row of lettuces he had planted. Then he heard a sound, a little high-pitched sound. He looked up. It seemed to be coming from the apple tree. There it was again, a tiny mewing sound, high up in the branches. He put down his spade and walked over to the tree. Something fluffy and black, with two large green eyes, was staring down at him.

4 ALL ABOARD – Ben and Sally were on holiday. One morning they walked down to the little beach near their holiday cottage. Jock the fisherman was sitting on a rock, mending a hole in his fishing net. There were some freshly caught mackerel in a bag by his feet. Nearby, bobbing gently on the waves, was his boat, *The Rainbow*. When he heard the children, Jock looked up. 'Fancy a bit of fishing, do you?', he asked.

5 THE PICNIC – Ben and Sally clambered over the rocks, till they came to their special secret beach. You couldn't see it from the road, and the only way to reach it was to go to the main beach and then find your way over the rocks. 'I'm starving,' said Ben, when they finally reached the little stretch of sand fringed by rock pools. They found a spot in the shade, and spread everything out on the ground.

Titles (1) *(continued)*

6 HARRY'S BAD DAY – Harry could hear a loud noise. He opened his eyes. The
noise was coming from Mum. It was saying 'Get up, we're late, hurry!' He
put his shoes on the wrong feet, dropped all his school things on the stairs,
and tipped over the box of cereal. When he got to school he realised he'd
forgotten his PE kit, so he had to stand and watch. At playtime he
accidentally tripped up Miss Chalk, and got sent in. The worst was when he
opened his lunch box and found he'd got his sister's lunch – tuna
sandwiches, yuk!

7 A LUCKY ESCAPE – Jack didn't want to go to school. It was Friday, and they
always had a spelling test on Fridays. Jack wasn't very good at spellings, and
worse than that, he'd forgotten to take the spelling list home, so he hadn't
learnt any of them. He felt fed up and worried as he walked into the school.
But when he got to his classroom, Miss Blot, his teacher was away. A supply
teacher called Miss Pansy was teaching his class, but she didn't realise it was
Friday, and did the Thursday timetable instead.

8 ZOO ADVENTURE – Nan and Grandpa took Zoe to the zoo for a treat in the
holidays. Zoe loved going to the zoo, and her favourite animals were the
monkeys. They went to the monkey house first, and Zoe and Ears, her fluffy
toy rabbit, stood laughing at the silly tricks. Then something awful
happened. One of the monkeys reached through the bars with its skinny arm
and snatched Ears right out of Zoe's hand. Zoe started to cry, and Nan went
to find the keeper. The keeper got inside the cage and chased round and
round, trying to rescue Ears from the naughty monkey. Finally the monkey
got tired of the game, and threw Ears up in the air. Ears flew over the fence
and landed on the ground right in front of Zoe.

Story Spotter (2)

GOLDILOCKS

Once upon a time there was a girl called Goldilocks. One bright sunny morning she decided to go for a walk. She climbed over the fence at the back of her garden, and walked down the path in the woods. After a while she came to a little cottage.

The door was wide open, and Goldilocks, who was a nosy little girl, peeped inside.

She could smell something delicious, and she saw three steaming bowls of porridge.

The following items should be ticked:

◆ Goldilocks
◆ The path through the trees
◆ The cottage in the trees
◆ The door
◆ The three bowls of porridge.

RED RIDING HOOD

Little Red Riding Hood lived in a cottage in the forest with her mum and dad. One day her mum asked her to take some food to Granny, because Granny was ill. She walked through the forest carrying the food in a basket. There were flowers growing beside the path, so she stopped to pick some. Something moved in the undergrowth, and a large grey wolf appeared. He walked up to Little Red Riding Hood and asked where she was going.

The following items should be ticked:

◆ Food for Granny
◆ Cottage in the woods
◆ Red Riding Hood walking with the basket
◆ The wolf
◆ Bunch of flowers.

  Speechmark Ⓟ

Story Spotter (2) *(continued)*

CINDERELLA
Cinderella lived with her father, her stepmother and her two ugly stepsisters.
One day, an invitation came to go to a ball at the Prince's palace. The stepsisters
said Cinderella couldn't go. They were always being mean and unkind to
Cinderella.
They went off to the ball and left Cinderella alone, feeling very sad. Suddenly
there was a puff of smoke and a strange-looking lady appeared.

The following items should be ticked:
◆ Cinderella's family
◆ The invitation
◆ The sisters shouting at Cinderella
◆ Cinderella alone and sad
◆ A puff of smoke
◆ The fairy godmother.

JACK AND THE BEANSTALK
Jack lived with his mum in a small cottage. One day, Jack's mum sent him off to
the market to try to sell their cow. When he got there, he met a funny old man,
who persuaded him to swap the cow for a handful of beans. Jack's mum was
furious when he arrived home with no cow, no money and a few beans. She
threw the beans out of the window and refused to make Jack any tea.

The following should be ticked:
◆ The cottage
◆ Jack leading the cow
◆ The funny old man
◆ Jack's angry mum
◆ The beans being thrown away.

Story Spotter (2) *(continued)*

Stage II

Getting the
Main Idea

Speechmark Ⓟ This page may be photocopied for instructional use only. *Speaking, Listening & Understanding*

Story Spotter (2) *(continued)*

Stage II

Getting the
Main Idea

Stage II

Story Spotter (2) *(continued)*

Getting the
Main Idea

Story Spotter (2) *(continued)*

Stage II

Getting the
Main Idea

Stage II

Getting the
Main Idea

Story Points (2)

The Painting

1 *Kim* decided to do some painting. She got a large sheet of *paper* and her box of *paints* and started to paint a butterfly. (3 points)
2 *Whisky the cat* sat on a *chair*, watching her. (2 points)
3 Just then a real *butterfly* came into the room. Whisky was on his feet immediately. *He leapt up at the butterfly* and missed. He ran forwards, then paused, his *four paws in the paint box.* (3 points)
4 Then he jumped at it again, and this time *he landed on the paper.* Poor Kim, her painting was covered with *brightly coloured cat prints.* (2 points)
5 *Kim sat* and thought for a bit. The *butterfly flew out of the window* and *Whisky went back to his chair.* (3 points)

TOTAL = 13 POINTS

The Picnic

1 *Lyndsay and Claire* were best friends. Lyndsay had *long blonde hair.* Claire had *black curly hair.* (3 points)
2 One day they decided to go for a picnic. They put *sandwiches, crisps* and *two bars of chocolate* in a *bag.* (4 points)
3 The walked down to the *river* and spread out a *rug* on the *ground.* (3 points)
4 Before they had their picnic, *they* decided to go and *look at the river.* They left the *bag on the rug.* (3 points)
5 When *they came back* to eat the picnic, they discovered the *bag was empty.* (2 points)

TOTAL = 15 POINTS

Speechmark ℗ *Speaking, Listening & Understanding*

Story Points (2) *(continued)*

Stage II

Getting the
Main Idea

The Key

1 *Carlos* was spending the weekend at his dad's new house. It was *raining* and he was bored. Dad and Karen had only just moved in and there were *boxes* all over the place. (3 points)

2 Dad and Karen were busy decorating the kitchen. Karen *stood on a stepladder, painting the ceiling. Dad painted the walls*. (3 points)

3 The *computer was still in its box*, so Carlos couldn't play on that. The *TV wouldn't work* because it needed a new aerial. Even *Scrap*, the dog, looked a bit fed up. (3 points)

4 Carlos decided to explore *upstairs*. He *went into the room* that was going to be 'his'. So far it just had a *bed* and a *small cupboard*. (4 points)

5 He *opened the cupboard*. It was empty, except for a *key*. Just then Carlos noticed *another door* in the room. (3 points)

TOTAL = 16 POINTS

The Pet

1 *Emma* wanted a pet of her own, but Mum said she couldn't have one. So she caught a *butterfly* and put it in a *jar*. (3 points)

2 Her brother *Tim* said it was cruel, so she let it *fly away* through the *open window*. (4 points)

3 Then she found a *frog* in the garden. She put it in a *box* and made *holes in the lid* so it could breathe. (3 points)

4 Her *dad* said it needed to be free, so she *let it go* near the pond. She sat and watched it *hop into the water*. (3 points)

5 Suddenly she heard a little sound coming from high up the *apple tree*. She *looked up*, and saw *something black and furry*. (3 points)

TOTAL = 16 points

Stage II

Getting the Main Idea

Story Points (2) *(continued)*

The Football Game

1 *Ben, Jake, Tom and Zak* were playing *football. Emma* wanted to join in, so she walked over to the pitch *with her football*. (7)

2 When she asked the boys if she could play, they just *laughed*, and said, *'No, we don't let soppy girls play with us'*! (2 points)

3 So *Emma stood watching*, feeling left out and fed up. *Zak stood in goal* as *Ben gave a huge kick*. Zak missed the ball completely, as *it went straight over the top of the net*. (4 points)

4 The children stood horrified, as they saw the *ball land right on top of a lorry*. The lorry driver had no idea what was happening, and *just carried on driving*, with their precious football on the back of his lorry! (2 points)

5 They turned sadly back to the football pitch. Then *they noticed Emma*. 'Emma', *called Ben*. 'Emma, do you want to come and play with us'? (2 points)

TOTAL = 17 POINTS

The Nest

1 *Tilak* lived in a flat with his *mum*. The flat was on the third floor, and there was a *big tree* outside the *window*. (4 points)

2 *Tilak* loved sitting on his bed *watching the tree*. There was a *blackbird's nest* with *three baby blackbirds* in it. The *parents* brought them *worms* to eat. (4 points)

3 One day Tilak and his mum were getting ready to go to Tilak's auntie's wedding. Mum put on her *best clothes,* and her *big hoop earrings*. Tilak wore a *shirt* and *tie* and black *trousers*. (5)

4 Mum couldn't find her gold bracelet anywhere. *Tilak* looked *under the bed,* and *behind the chair*. *Mum* looked in all the *drawers*, but it wasn't there. (4 points)

5 *Tilak* got bored with looking, and went to *look out of the window*. The blackbird's *nest was empty* now that the baby birds had flown away. But something caught Tilak's eye. (3 points)

TOTAL 20 POINTS

Stories in Disguise

Stage II

Getting the
Main Idea

These stories are only part written, because experience has shown that children are usually very quick to work out the real story. However, if by the end of the text they haven't got it, you will have to continue ad libbing!

1 I heard a story about this guy who was out of work. He had an old motorbike that needed new tyres. One day his mum told him to sell the bike, so he went down to the garage. The owner was busy with another customer, so he had to wait for ages. While he was waiting, this camper van pulled up. A bloke with long dreadlocks and a red T-shirt covered in stars got out. He had an eyebrow stud and tattoos on his arms. He looked at the bike, and came over and said 'Man, that's a cool bike. Tell you what, how about swapping it for these amazing plants I've got in the back of the van?' Well, Jack (that's his name, by the way), thought for a minute, then he said, 'OK then'. You can imagine what his mum said, when he arrived home with a couple of flower pots and no bike!

(Jack and the Beanstalk)

2 This story is about a girl who lived with her parents on the edge of a large town. She didn't have any brothers or sisters, but she had lots of friends at school. Her parents both worked hard during the week, and on Sundays they liked to get up late. It was a summer Sunday morning, and she woke up quite early. Mum and Dad were fast asleep, so she went downstairs and watched TV for a bit. Then she looked outside – it was a lovely day. She decided to go out for a bit. She put on her trainers and went out of the back door. There was a playing field at the back of the house, and beyond it a wood. She wasn't allowed to go in that wood, only on the playing field. But it was such a nice day, and the wood looked green and inviting. So she climbed over the gate and started to walk along the path. At the end of the path was a house, which she'd never noticed before.

(Goldilocks)

3 A long time ago there was a rich man and his wife. They had a daughter, and sadly, when the girl was about 12 years old, her mother died. About a year later her dad married again and they went to live in the new wife's house with her and her daughters. It was a very grand house, in the smart part of town. The daughters were only interested in fashion, and who was seen with who. Their main ambition was to get a rich husband, and their mother made sure they got asked to all the right parties. There was a really important party at the end of the week, and they were already fussing about what to wear. Their stepsister usually got left out of these conversations, and if they included her it was only to run errands for them, or tell them they looked amazing. She hated doing this because they were both overweight, and usually looked awful in their too-tight little tops and skirts.

(Cinderella)

Stage II

Getting the
Main Idea

Stories in Disguise *(continued)*

4 King Harold and Queen Beatrice lived with their daughter, the Princess Melissa, in a beautiful castle. Princess Melissa had a great life. She didn't have any brothers or sisters, but she played with the servants' children. The castle was a brilliant place for all kinds of games, and the grown ups let them do what they wanted most of the time. One day Melissa was a bit bored. All the servants' children had gone on a trip to the beach, organised every year by the King and Queen. Melissa went into Queen Beatrice's office, to see if her mum was busy. But the Queen wasn't there, so she walked across the office and through the door on the other side. This led into another office, where a woman was busy working at a computer. Page after page was coming out of the printer, and every so often she had to stop typing and staple some of the pages together. She noticed Melissa come into the room, and muttered, 'I'm never going to get all this done today. I told her I needed more help and she just wouldn't listen!' So Melissa asked if she could help in any way. 'You can staple the sheets together for me, that would be a great help,' said the woman. She handed Melissa the stapler and the sheets of paper. Melissa had to work quickly to keep up with the printer, and in her hurry she got her finger caught in the stapler and one of the staples went under her skin. 'Ouch,' she exclaimed. Then everything began to swim in front of her, and suddenly she felt very, very sleepy. She laid her head down on the table, and in seconds, was fast asleep.

(Sleeping Beauty)

5 Lisa lived with her mum and dad in a small village. Her dad worked at the sawmill, and her mum was a hairdresser. Lisa's nan lived at the other end of the street, past the playground. Lisa liked going round to Nan's because she had lots of interesting ornaments, and she always had some sweets for Lisa. Nan couldn't walk very well since she fell over on the ice, so Lisa's mum did her shopping for her. One morning, Mum went to Tesco's to get the shopping. When she came back she asked Lisa to take it round to Nan's. It was a really cold morning, so Lisa put on her red fleece and set off with the blue-and-white-striped Tesco bag. When she got to the playground she saw some of her friends playing on the swings, and she wanted to go and join them. She put the Tesco bag down, but a very large, grey dog came up and sniffed at it. So she decided she'd better take the shopping to Nan's first. The dog lolloped along beside her. It really was huge, with grey spiky fur and no collar. It was panting and Lisa could see its pointed teeth. Suddenly it bounded off, in the direction of Nan's house.

(Red Riding Hood)

Story Spotter (3)

Stage III

Getting the
Main Idea

1 There was once a boy called Ben, who lived with his Dad in a small village.
Ben really wanted a dog, but Dad said they couldn't have one because they
were out at work and school all day.

While they were watching TV together, Ben heard a scratching noise. He
went into the kitchen to see what it was. He could hear something
scratching at the back door. Dad came to see what it was. When he opened
the door, they saw a little black and white puppy on the doorstep. Dad said
they had to find out who the puppy belonged to, so they went to the police
station.

The puppy belonged to old Mr Smart, who lived next door to Ben and his
dad. They took the puppy back to Mr Smart, and Mr Smart asked Ben if he
would take the puppy for a walk every day. Ben was really happy. It was
nearly as good as having a dog of his own.

2 Many years ago there was a dragon called Max. Max lived in dark, gloomy
cave high up in the mountains. He lived by himself and he was very lonely.
He was sitting looking out of his cave at the mountains one summer
evening, when he saw something very small and shiny. It was flying towards
the cave. Max kept very still and watched the little creature. It landed on the
ground in front of him. It was dressed in sparkling green clothes, and on its
back were bright red wings. The creature looked up at Max, and then
covered up its eyes.

'I won't hurt you,' said Max. 'Come and have a cup of tea'. The little
creature peeped up at Max, and started to cry. 'I'm lost, and I'm lonely,' it
said. Max smiled for the first time in about a hundred years. Then he asked
the little creature to come and live with him and be his friend. They lived
happily together in the cave for a long time.

Stage III

Getting the
Main Idea

Story Spotter (3) *(continued)*

3 Eve was very excited. Mum and Dad gave her a green bike for her birthday.
Dad said she could ride down to the shop on it as long as she kept on the
pavement. She waved to him and started to pedal. Dad walked along behind.
Eve was so busy working the pedals that she didn't look where she was going
and she ran into the back of Mr Smart's legs. Mr Smart was very cross. He
shouted, 'Just look where you're going, young lady!' Eve started to cry, but
Dad said, 'Come on, Eve, I've got a good idea.' He picked up the bike and
they went home. Dad went into the shed, and looked in a box. He found a
horn, got out his tools, and fixed it to the bike. They tried it out, and it
worked brilliantly. So Eve set off again, with Dad walking beside her. She saw
the boy from the shop, carrying a big box of eggs. It was so big he couldn't
see over the top of it, so Eve beeped her horn. 'BEEP, BEEP!' The sound was
so loud that it gave the boy a shock and he dropped the box of eggs!

4 It was Saturday morning. Tom had his friend Nassim over, and they were
playing with his new Lego® set. Tom's little sister, Amy, wanted to play, but
she was annoying the boys. In the end, Tom said she could go into the
bathroom and play with his red boat. Amy trotted off, looking pleased. She
climbed into the dry bath and put the plug in. Then she climbed out and
turned on the cold tap. Once there was enough water the boat sailed
beautifully. A bit later, Dad called the children down for lunch. As they sat
eating their chicken nuggets and chips, a drop of water landed on Mum's
plate. Then another, and another. Everyone looked up. A large wet patch
had appeared on the ceiling. Dad rushed upstairs. Tom and Nassim looked at
Amy. Dad opened the bathroom door. The water sloshed around his feet,
and as he tried to get to the tap, he slipped and ended up sitting in the
water.

Story Spotter (3) *(continued)*

Stage III

Getting the Main Idea

Stage III

Story Spotter (3) *(continued)*

Getting the Main Idea

Story Spotter (3) *(continued)*

Stage III

Getting the
Main Idea

Stage III

Getting the Main Idea

Story Spotter (3) *(continued)*

Who's Got The Key?

Stage III

Getting the Main Idea

Suggestions for objects are listed at the end of each story. These can be altered according to what is available, but should obviously include the 'key' object, which is in italic. Add objects as necessary, depending on the size of the group.

1 Tim was in the supermarket with his mum. He was very fed up because he hated shopping. He wanted to go skateboarding with his friends, but instead he had to trudge up and down the aisles, and then wait for ages at the checkout. While he was standing at the checkout, he noticed a poster advertising a colouring competition. The first prize was a Playstation 2. He took home a copy of the poster and got busy.
(book, rubber, *packet of crayons*, pair of scissors, sock, paper clip)

2 Carly was on her way to meet her friend in the park. It was a sunny day, and she had a drink and a bar of chocolate in her pocket. At the entrance to the park, she noticed something in the grass. It was a silver bracelet with someone's initials engraved on it. Just then Carly's friend Gemma appeared. They looked at the bracelet, then Gemma said they should really take it to the police station. When they got there the policeman on duty said that only that morning a lady had come in offering a reward for anyone who found her silver bracelet – a reward of £10! The two girls were very glad they had decided to be honest, and they shared the reward money.
(10p coin, glove, purse, watch, *bracelet*, sheet of paper with 'REWARD! – £10!' written on it)

Stage III

Getting the Main Idea

Who's Got The Key? *(continued)*

3 One cold winter afternoon, Ben went for a walk with his dad and Rags, their dog. Ben threw an old ball for Rags, who loved charging after it and bringing it back, over and over again. As they came to the duck pond, Rags started barking. Dad and Ben went over to the pond to see what he was barking at. A young puppy was struggling in the water, trying to swim and swallowing a lot of water. Ben thought quickly, then tore off his scarf and threw one end of it towards the puppy. The puppy caught hold of it with his teeth, and Ben pulled him towards the edge of the pond. He scrambled out of the water, and showed his appreciation at being rescued by shaking all over Ben and his dad!
(*scarf*, glove, book, dog's lead, ball, teddy)

4 Leroy was walking home from school one day, when he noticed a white van outside the TV shop. Two men were carrying big boxes out of the shop and loading up the van. Another man sat at the steering wheel, drumming his fingers impatiently. As Leroy walked past, the driver's mobile rang and Leroy heard him say, 'We've nearly shifted it all, there's no one about, apart from a kid.' Leroy began to feel suspicious. He glanced over his shoulder and caught sight of the number plate of the van, NIK 123. In his pocket was a felt pen and a pencil. He scribbled the number on his hand with the felt pen and walked quickly home to ask his mum what he should do.
(pencil, book, *felt pen*, key, glove, purse)

Speechmark **P** *Speaking, Listening & Understanding*
© C Delamain & J Spring 2003

What's She On About?

Write out the word lists in large lettering on separate sheets of paper, one for each text. Other simple pieces of non-fiction text can be adapted, using the same format.

Stage IV

Getting the
Main Idea

1 It is extremely important for children to learn how to cross the road safely.
   Lots of children are too busy playing or chatting to their friends to think
   about the traffic. They would rather be looking at their Pokemon cards or
   playing on their Gameboys. Many accidents could be avoided if children
   knew more about the dangers of not paying attention to what is going on
   around them.
   Word List: Pokemon, friends, *road safety*, or cars

2 If you look in a pond early in spring you may find some frogspawn. Other
   living creatures will begin to come out of hibernation too, like water beetles
   and newts. Frogs often return to the same pond to lay their eggs. The
   tadpoles soon hatch out and start swimming around. A lot of them will be
   eaten by fish in the pond, or by birds before they grow legs and turn into
   frogs.
   Word List: frogs, newts, spring, *tadpoles*

3 There are lots of famous buildings in London, such as Big Ben, the Houses of
   Parliament, Buckingham Palace, and the Tower of London. The River Thames
   flows through the city, and visitors like to take a boat ride down the river.
   London is famous for its bright red buses, and the guards with their furry
   black helmets, who stand outside Buckingham Palace. The streets of central
   London are very crowded and busy, and it is a relief to sit in one of the
   parks, away from the traffic.
   Word List: *London*, Buckingham Palace, River Thames, Big Ben

Stage IV

Getting the Main Idea

What's She On About? *(continued)*

4 Oranges are delicious, juicy fruits, which grow on trees in warm countries. When they are ripe they are picked and sent all over the world. Next time you eat an orange, keep some of the pips. Get a little flower pot, and put some soil in it. Push the pips about 5 cm deep in the soil. Then get a small plastic bag and wrap it around the pot. This will keep the soil warm and moist. In a few weeks, tiny shoots will appear. Put the plant on a light windowsill, and remember to water it . After a while you will have your own little orange tree. You can try planting other pips too, like grapefruits, lemons and clementines.
Word List: oranges, gardening, *growing oranges*, flower pots.

5 In the summer it's great to be outside, playing in the warm sunshine. Everything looks better on a sunny day, and people feel happy. Playing too long in the sun can be dangerous though, and it's important to put on sun-cream if you want to play outside. If you don't wear sun-cream, you may get burnt, which is very painful. So, enjoy those lovely summer days outside. Have fun with your friends in the garden, in the park, on the beach. But don't forget the sun-cream!
Word List: summer, *sun-cream*, holidays, sunburn

6 Otters are very good swimmers. They have webbed feet. Their fur is smooth and waterproof. Otters feed mostly on fish, which they catch in the river. They have sharp teeth and claws. If you see an otter, you are lucky because they are very shy. They live in a kind of burrow built in the river bank, often under tree roots. Baby otters are called cubs. The cubs learn to swim when they are about 10 weeks old. They soon learn to dive and play in the water.
Word List: *Otters*, rivers, cubs, fish

Titles (2)

1 Lucy and Sam were on holiday by the seaside. They made a huge sandcastle
on the beach and decorated it with shells and bits of seaweed. Dad said he
wanted to take a photo of them standing by their castle. He held his camera
up to his eye and told them to smile. Then he took a step backwards, not
noticing the rock pool just behind him. The next thing he knew he was
sitting down, soaking wet in the pool. Poor Dad!
(Look Where You're Going, The Sandcastle, The Holiday)

2 Tom woke up late. His mum was shouting that he was late for school. He
couldn't find his clothes, and he knocked over his glass of water. When he
got downstairs his sister laughed at him because he had put on his
sweatshirt inside out. He had to run to catch the school bus, and when it
arrived it drove through a big puddle and splashed him.
(The School Bus, Late Again, Tom Goes to School)

3 Ben and Simon went to the zoo with their nan. It was a really hot day, so Nan
bought them an ice-cream each. Ben had a strawberry one and Simon had a
chocolate one. Both boys like the monkeys best and they stood as close to the
monkey cage as they could, laughing at the baby monkeys chasing each other.
Ben was so busy looking at them, he didn't notice a big, grown-up monkey
stretching its skinny arm through the bars and grabbing his ice-cream.
(Ben and the Monkey, A Hot Day, The Monkey Thief)

4 Laura and Zoe were very excited because the fair was in town. They couldn't
wait for the end of school. At last it was home time, and they rushed home,
changed and went with their auntie to the fair. They had a go on all the rides,
and then went round the different stalls. Zoe really wanted to win a huge
fluffy dolphin, but she had used up all her pocket money on the dodgems.
Luckily, Auntie Sue found 10p in her coat pocket. Zoe had one more go, and
this time she managed to get the hoop right on top of the target. She
proudly carried home her prize, whom she decided to call Flapper.
(Flapper the Dolphin, Fun on the Dodgems, Zoe's Lucky Day)

5 Every day Sam walked to school with his mum and his baby sister. On the way
they went past a field with a donkey in it. The donkey would come up to the
fence, and if there was time, Mum would let Sam pat its nose. One day the
donkey wasn't there. Sam was sad, and his little sister cried, 'Want donk-donk!'
Mum didn't know where the donkey was, but she said maybe it was in its little
stable. Next day Sam had a great surprise. When they got to the donkey field,
there wasn't just one donkey, but there was a little baby one as well!
(Sam's Journey to School, The Friendly Donkey, The Donkey Surprise)

Story Spotter (4)

1 Kim's Nan knitted Kim a jumper for her birthday. It was all different coloured stripes, and made of really soft wool. Kim was very pleased with it, and wore it every day for the whole of the half-term holiday. Mum said she must let her wash it, so Kim put the jumper in the washing machine, ready for the next wash. Mum was very busy changing the sheets, and she bundled the white ones into the machine without looking inside. Then she switched it to HOT, and turned it on. Oh dear! When she took it out, Kim's jumper had shrunk. It was tiny, far too small for Kim to wear. Kim had a good idea – once the jumper had dried it was just the right size for her teddy!

2 Wayne and Lee were bored. It was the summer holidays, and they couldn't think of anything to do. Wayne suggested going to the park, but Lee didn't want to because his big brother would be there with his friends, and they always teased Lee. So they went round to Wayne's and hung about in his back garden. It wasn't much of a garden really, because Wayne's dad kept his motorbikes in it. He had three bikes, which he was always mending and fiddling around with. At the end of the garden was a shed with a broken door. Lee and Wayne went and leant against the shed, trying to think of something exciting to do. Then Lee noticed something in the hedge. Something round. He nudged Wayne and pointed. They walked over to the hedge and knelt down. It looked like a huge egg, nearly as big as a rugby ball. The shell was pale green with some darker green smudges on it. As they watched, a tiny crack appeared, and gradually grew bigger and bigger.

Story Spotter (4) *(continued)*

Stage IV

Getting the
Main Idea

3 Sophie and Vicky were on holiday by the sea. They were staying in a caravan with Sophie's mum and her little brother, Rob. The caravan park was really near the beach, and Sophie and Vicky spent all day playing on the sand, or looking in the rock pools for crabs and little fish. One day they decided to make a mermaid. They drew out the shape on the sand. Then they collected some seaweed to make the hair. They used shells to make eyes, nose and a mouth, and a different kind of seaweed for the fishy tail. 'I think we should call her Ella,' said Sophie, standing back to admire her work. They spent a happy afternoon making up stories about Ella and her underwater adventures. But then they noticed the tide coming in, and watched sadly as Ella was swept under the waves. The next morning the two girls went down to the beach to look for crabs. As they crouched by a large rock pool they heard the sound of singing. It was a tiny, high-pitched voice, and they couldn't tell where it was coming from. Suddenly Sophie gasped. She grabbed Vicky's arm and pointed. 'Look!' she whispered. 'Over there on that rock!' The two girls stared in amazement, as they watched a tiny mermaid sitting on a rock, combing her long black hair.

4 Josh was upset. He couldn't find Tig anywhere. Tig was his toy cat, and Josh took him everywhere. Tig was black with white paws and a red collar. He was in a permanent sitting position, and Josh liked to sit him on the shelf by his bed, like a real cat. They couldn't have a real cat in the flat, because it said 'no pets'. That's what Mum said anyway, but Josh secretly thought Mum didn't want a real cat. He looked everywhere for Tig. He remembered having him the day before, when they walked down the road to Nan's. But Mum phoned Nan, and she said she'd looked everywhere, and he wasn't at her house. Josh wanted to go and look at Nan's himself, and he begged Mum to let him. She wouldn't let him walk down the road on his own, so he had to wait until she had time. It seemed a very long day, but at last they set off. They went past the shop, and Josh didn't even ask for sweets. Old Mr Potts was in his garden, planting seeds. He stopped to say hello to Mum. As usual, it wasn't just hello, it turned into a proper chat. Josh was getting restless, so he climbed on the fence and looked into Mr Pott's garden. Then he had the surprise of his life – there, sitting up straight, in the middle of Mr Pott's vegetable patch, was Tig! Josh shouted to Mum, and she and Mr Potts looked round. 'Oh dear, is he yours?' asked Mr Potts. 'He's doing a grand job scaring the birds off my seeds!'

Stage IV

Getting the
Main Idea

Story Spotter (4) (continued)

Story Spotter (4) *(continued)*

Stage IV

Getting the Main Idea

PAGE 235

Stage IV

Getting the
Main Idea

Story Spotter (4) *(continued)*

Story Spotter (4) *(continued)*

Stage IV

Getting the Main Idea

Birthday Party

New Clothes

Stage III

Thinking
Skills

Mrs Fusspot says 'No thank you, I don't like silly big bows.'

'I don't like checks, thank you, don't show me any more of those.'

'Oh I love flowers. But I'm scared of spiders, I don't want *them* on my dress!'

'That plain one's a bit boring. I like a bit of interest on my clothes!!'

'I'm not keen on stripes. They make me look like a zebra.'

'No, no short sleeves. My arms are too fat.'

'No, short skirts aren't for me. I always wanted nice legs, but…!'

'Oh dear, I'm sorry, I can't stand spotty materials.'

Stage III

Thinking
Skills

New Clothes *(continued)*

Speechmark P This page may be photocopied for instructional use only. *Speaking, Listening & Understanding*
© C Delamain & J Spring 2003

Swift Solutions!

Examples:

The cat is on the table near the butter dish.

A child can't reach the letterbox to post a card.

You can't reach the cupboard.

A bottle of milk has tipped over and made a puddle.

None of the pencils in the classroom pot have a point on them.

A new child at school doesn't know where to hang his coat.

You are feeling thirsty, and Mum is upstairs.

You haven't got enough money for the sweets that you want in the shop.

Your favourite jumper is in the wash.

Your bike has a puncture.

You are bored with the TV programme you are watching.

Stage III

Thinking
Skills

First Things First

Mum is doing some cooking. Something is burning in the oven, the phone is ringing, and the postman has just knocked on the door.

A lady has reached the checkout and there are several people in the queue behind her. She has pushed the baby buggy past the checkout. The baby is crying. The lady realises she has to go back into the shop for some cereal.

A girl has dropped her school bag and some things have fallen out of it on the pavement. The lollipop lady has just stopped the traffic to help the children cross the road.

A boy has lost his dad in a large store. As he is going up the escalator to look for him, he sees his dad coming down on the other escalator.

Mandy's budgie is having some exercise outside his cage. Mandy suddenly sees that the window is open and the cat is sitting behind the sofa, licking his lips.

Clues

Suspects: A woman with a handbag. A boy on a bike. A man with a dog.
Clue: A dropped lipstick.

Suspects: A boy on a bike. A man with a dog. An old lady with a basket of shopping.
Clue: A till receipt.

Suspects: A woman with a bunch of flowers. A girl with a doll in a pram.
A man with a mobile phone.
Clue: Some rose petals.

Suspects: A boy with an Action Man®. A woman with a baby in a pram. An old man with a walking stick.
Clue: A rattle.

Suspects: A woman with a pile of library books. A man reading a letter. A girl eating an ice-cream.
Clue: A torn envelope.

Suspects: A boy eating chewing gum. A girl eating an ice-cream. A man in overalls carrying a bag of tools.
Clue: Some crushed wafer.

Suspects: A man carrying a bag of tools. A boy in a tracksuit and trainers.
A woman with a packet of letters to post.
Clue: Some oil on the door.

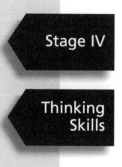

Stage IV

Thinking Skills

Bizzo

Below are Bizzo's 'alien words' and their meanings. You can make up more words and text as required.

jigga	jumper
plimper	spoon
figgle	phone
cratiator	park
snozdrogs	football
scop	buy
jimmer	house

Bizzo got up early in the morning. He opened his cupboard and chose his favourite *jigga*. He pulled it over his head and put his arms in the sleeves.

He went downstairs feeling really hungry. He got out a bowl and filled it with Spacepops. Then he poured on some milk and rather a lot of sugar. He opened the drawer and got out a *plimper*, and sat down to eat his breakfast.

After breakfast he decided to phone his friend Jo. He picked up the *figgle* and dialled. When Jo answered, Bizzo asked him to meet him at the *cratiator* for a game of football.

They played *snozdrogs* for a bit, then they felt hungry. They went to the shop on the corner to *scop* some sweets. Jo asked Bizzo back to his *jimmer* to play on the playstation.

Jo's mum came back from the shop with some chocolate ice-cream. The boys got a bowl and a *plimper* each and soon there was hardly any ice-cream left. 'I think it's time you went back to your *jimmer*, Bizzo,' said Jo's mum.

Bus Driver

Stage IV

Thinking Skills

Checkout Chat

Stage I

Drawing
Inference

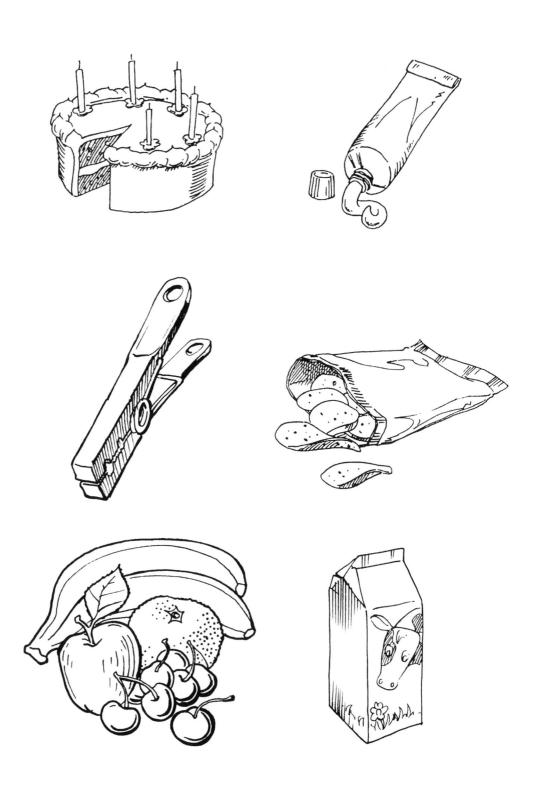

Speechmark **P** This page may be photocopied for instructional use only. *Speaking, Listening & Understanding*
© C Delamain & J Spring 2003

Last Words

Stage I

Drawing Inference

Situations

Charlie has been pinching some apples from Farmer Brown's apple tree. He is still up the tree when he hears Farmer Brown coming. *Charlie feels ...*

Charlie is waiting outside Father Christmas's grotto. *Charlie feels ...*

Charlie is late for the school bus. He can't find his PE kit. *Charlie feels ...*

Charlie is having his birthday party. All his friends are there, and he has been given lots of presents. *Charlie feels ...*

Charlie is looking for his shoes. He is sure he left them under his bed, but they aren't there now. *Charlie feels ...*

Charlie wants to go for a bike ride, but his mate won't come with him. *Charlie feels ...*

The family was planning to go on a trip to Alton Towers, but now they can't go because the car has broken down. *Charlie feels ...*

Charlie sees some big boys hurting a dog. *Charlie feels ...*

Charlie's teacher is reading a story, but Charlie has heard this story lots of times before. *Charlie feels ...*

Charlie's hamster has died. *Charlie feels ...*

Stage I

Drawing Inference

Think About It

Emma is in a shop with her mum. She has only one shoe on, and she is sitting on a chair. There are several boxes on the floor around her.

Where is Emma?
What is she doing?

Ben is sitting on a chair in front of a mirror. There is a man standing behind him with a pair of scissors and a comb.

Where is Ben?
Who can he see in the mirror?

Kylie is looking at a picture on a piece of folded card. There is a number three on the picture. Kylie is smiling.

What is Kylie looking at?
How old is she?

Mum put sandwiches, crisps and a drink in two plastic boxes. The boys put the boxes in the sports bag, with their swimming things. 'Hurry up or you'll miss the bus,' said Mum.

Where are they going?
Are they going to walk?
How do you know they are over eight years old?

It was due to start at seven o'clock. They stood waiting, stamping their feet with cold. Suddenly there was a 'Whoosh!' Everybody looked up into the night sky and saw the sparks, all different colours. The next one was a banger and some of the younger children were frightened.

What were they watching?
What time of year was it?
What was the weather like?

Think About It *(continued)*

Stage I

Drawing
Inference

Ben stopped and got out. 'I must have gone over a nail or something,' he said to his friend Tim. Tim said he could fix it. 'Will it take long?' said Ben. 'I'm already late for work.' Tim did the job in five minutes and they set off again.

What had happened to the car?
Does Ben know how to change a wheel?
Are they travelling by bicycle or car?
How do you know Ben is in a hurry?

'That should be enough,' said Mum, putting the last sandwich on the plate. Then she stuck sticks in the little sausages. There were too many for one plate, so she got out another. She opened the fridge and took out a tray with 12 little dishes of jelly.

What is Mum getting ready for?
How many people are coming?
Are they children or adults?

Mum told Nassim that he would get double pocket money if he cleaned out the garden shed. 'That means I'll have £2,' he thought. While he did the job he thought about his collection. He would soon have enough money to get the comic with the new packet in it, and if he hurried he'd be able to get it before the shop shut.

How much pocket money did Nassim get?
Did he live near a shop?
Did he collect Beanie Babies or stickers?

Stage I

Drawing
Inference

Riddle Race

It's made of china, has a handle, but is not a jug. (A cup.)

It's got four feet, a long tail and it squeaks. (A mouse.)

It has wings, scales and breathes fire. (A dragon.)

They are made of glass, people wear them, but you can't drink out of them. (Glasses.)

It's made of wax and you can light it. (A candle.)

It's made of metal and it can fly, but it is not alive. (A plane.)

It has bristle, a handle and you can make pictures with it. (A paintbrush.)

It floats and people can travel in it. (A boat.)

It's full of water, which moves but never runs out. (A river.)

It grows, has a trunk, but cannot move. (A tree.)

Lost Property

Stage II

Drawing Inference

Possessions

hair dryer, glasses, scarf, glove, watch, carrot, whistle, umbrella.

Characters

Josh's nan always knits him something for his birthday.

Kelly is 15 and is always trying new hair styles.

Mr Carter always wins a prize in the best vegetable competition.

Terry Black is a referee for the local football team.

Old Mrs Trim gets very cold hands in the winter.

Dan is seven and has just learnt to tell the time.

Miss Jones always walks to work, whatever the weather.

Mr Gardner went to the optician's last week because he couldn't see the pictures in the newspaper.

Jamilla has a long train journey to work and she reads to pass the time.

Harry Higgs is going to enter his photos in a competition.

Josh got a Playstation 2 for Christmas.

Josh's nan always knits him a jumper for his birthday.

Stage II

Lost Property *(continued)*

Drawing
Inference

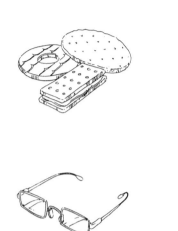

Speechmark ⑤ Ⓟ This page may be photocopied for instructional use only. *Speaking, Listening & Understanding*

Wacko's Wand

Stage II

Drawing
Inference

The suggested 'clues' are in brackets at the end of each description.

Biff Bruiser. Biff is very tall, and works in a quarry heaving enormous lumps of rock out of the ground, and loading them on to lorries. He gets very dirty doing this job, and also very hungry, so he usually has a few large bars of chocolate in his pockets. (chocolate wrapper)

Alice Finlay is tall and very thin. She has long curly hair, which is a very striking shade of red. Her finger nails are also very long and red. Alice writes books for children, and lives with her grey cat, Pixie. (a long red hair)

Violet Small is getting quite old now. She can't walk very far, and has to wear glasses, perched on the end of her hooked nose. Violet is extremely fond of baking, and is famous for her delicious gingerbread. (pair of glasses)

Geoff Jones owns The Golden Cauldron, which is Wacko's local pub. He smokes a pipe all the time, and whistles while he washes up the beer glasses. He likes horse racing, and usually has a copy of the *Racing Post* in his pocket. (pipe)

Melissa Mercury is a reporter for the *Wizard Gazette*. She has short blonde hair, and wears a leather coat. She drives a sports car, loves jewellery, and always carries a notebook in her bag. She is very fond of peppermint creams. (an earring, a notebook)

Bob Luck plays the drums in a band. He drives a big old van, and keeps his drums in the back. He often goes round to Wacko's with the rest of the band, because Wacko likes music. He's no good at cooking, but he loves pot noodles. (drum stick, empty pot noodle carton)

Stage II

Drawing
Inference

Wacko's Wand

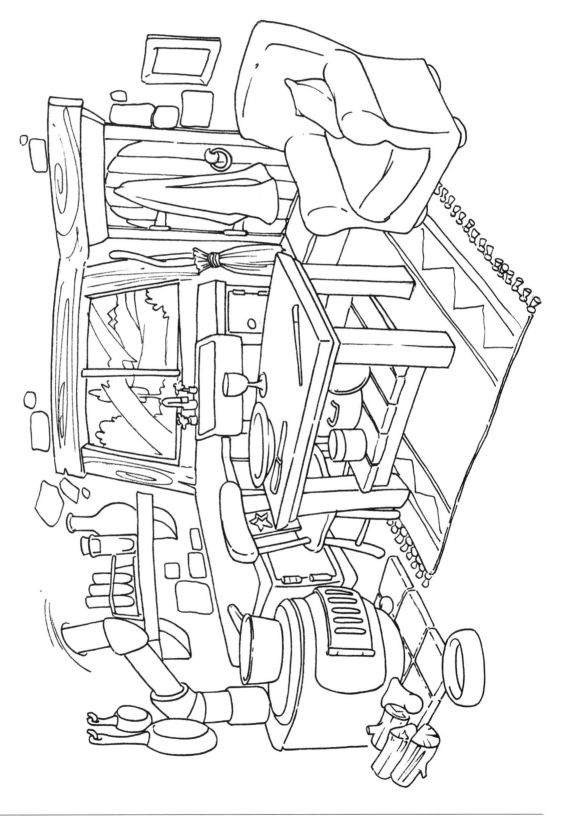

Weather Forecast

Stage II

Drawing
Inference

Sentences:

1 Dad said, 'My goodness, the sky looks dark. Time to get the sledge out of the garage.'

2 Mum said, 'Don't forget your sun hats and dark glasses, if you're going to be out for a long time.'

3 Dad said, 'I just hope that old tree doesn't come down in the night.'

4 Mum said, 'Can you get the cat in, you remember how frightened he was last time?'

5 Dad said, 'It might be a good day to try flying your new kite.'

6 Mum said, 'I believe there's an old pair of skates somewhere that might fit you.'

7 Dad said, 'How about a picnic if this weather lasts?'

8 Mum said, 'If this keeps up all night, the garden will look so pretty in the morning.'

9 Dad said, 'The most tremendous bang woke us up, and now it sounds as if it's right overhead.'

10 Mum said, 'Please can you put some fresh water on the bird-table, the lot I put out yesterday will be solid by now.'

Stage II

Drawing
Inference

Rover and the Vet

1 Your dog needs to go on a diet. (fat dog)

2 You need to give this dog some extra food. (thin dog)

3 You should keep your dog on a lead when you are going through the farm. (dog chasing sheep)

4 This dog needs to wear a muzzle when you are out. (dog biting other dog)

5 You should take this dog to dog-training classes. (dog pulling hard on lead)

6 You need to buy some flea powder. (dog scratching itself violently)

7 Try getting him some chewy bones to play with instead. (dog destroying slipper)

8 Try feeding him at a different time. (dog eating cat's food as well as his own, while cat watches)

Rover and the Vet *(continued)*

Stage II

Drawing Inference

Stage III

Drawing
Inference

Animal Lotto

Box 1: 'Bother that animal,' said Mum. 'He left his bone lying about on the stairs again and I nearly fell over it.'

Box 2: 'You've forgotten to feed Percy again this morning,' said Mum. 'He's hunting about at the bottom of the tank and he can't find a scrap of food.'

Box 3: John said he'd found tiny teeth marks in the larder.

Box 4: 'Come quick,' Susie called Dad. 'Tigger is up a tree and I don't think he can get down.'

Box 5: Mum said, 'Gran's coming this afternoon with her long-handled broom. She'll get those cobwebs down.'

Box 6: James saw lots of little broken egg shells under the bush outside the window.

Box 7: 'Look,' called Ben. 'There's farmer Giles chasing down the road. One got away when they were coming back from the milking shed.'

Box 8: Uncle Jim got out his binoculars. He could hear it twittering but he couldn't spot it.

Animal Lotto *(continued)*

Stage IIII

Drawing Inference

Stage III

Drawing
Inference

Dan's Day Out

Story 1: The Theme Park

Dan was going out for the day with his Mum and Dad. His eyes sparkled and he sang a little song to himself as he ate his breakfast. (How was he feeling? Do you think they are going somewhere nice, or not? Sort out the suggestions, which should include 'excited', and then continue with the story.)

They were going to a Theme Park where there were animals, rides, a playground, and a Ghost Train. After breakfast, they got in the car and set out. After about half an hour Dan began to wonder how much longer it was going to be, and wish he had brought something to read or to play with. (How was he feeling? *Bored.*)

At last they got to the park. Dad paid, and they decided they would go and visit the animals first. Dan stood outside one of the cages. His heart beat rather quickly and his hair felt as if it was standing on end. (*Nervous, scared.*)

At last the huge lion standing just inside the wire blinked his eyes, licked his lips, and stalked off. Dan heaved a sigh of relief. He had felt sure that somehow that lion was going to get over the fence, he had looked so fierce and angry. They visited the elephants, the giraffes, the penguins and the sea lions. The sea lions were having their morning feed. Dan watched intently as the keeper picked a fish out of his bucket, and tossed it carefully to one of the animals. The sea lions were brilliant at catching! (How was he feeling? *Interested, fascinated.*)

After the animals, Dad asked Dan if he wanted to go on any of the rides. Dan chose the Big Dipper, and decided he would go alone, while Dad watched. It was tremendously exciting as they swooped and dived up and down, and it sometimes felt as if they were dropping right out of the sky. When Dan got off his face was rather pale and sweaty, and he had a hand on his tummy. (*Sick.*) Dad asked him if he was alright, and gave him a mint which made him feel a lot better.

The rest of the day passed in a flash. They had a brilliant lunch of beefburgers and chips, went on the Ghost Train, and Dad won an enormous teddy in the shooting range. At last it was time to go home. Almost before they were out of the gate Dan felt his eyelids drooping and he gave a mighty yawn. (*Tired, sleepy.*)

'Don't you dare go to sleep', Mum said, 'or you'll never sleep tonight when you get to bed.' But it was no good. Dan was out for the count, and slept through most of the journey.

Dan's Day Out

Stage III

Drawing Inference

Story 2: Dan Goes to Hospital

Dan woke when it was only just light that Tuesday morning. He lay in bed and wondered why he had woken so early. Then he remembered. It was the morning he was going into hospital to have his tonsils out. It all came back to him in a rush. (How did he feel? *Nervous, scared, frightened, anxious.*) He swallowed carefully to see if his throat was sore. He knew that if it was, they wouldn't do the operation. (*Hopeful, anxious.*) But it seemed perfectly all right, unfortunately. (*Disappointed, cross.*)

He got up and went downstairs. Mum was in the kitchen making cups of tea. 'Can I have a really super breakfast, to make up for going into hospital?' Dan asked. 'Sorry,' Mum said, 'Don't you remember you can't have anything to eat before your operation? You can have a drink of water, though.' (*Furious, hungry, horrified.*) When everyone else had had their tea and some breakfast, Mum and Dan got into the car. The rest of the family stood by the door to wave and wish him luck. (*Nervous, scared, important.*)

Once they got to the hospital, everything seemed to happen at once, and Dan could hardly keep track of it. First he had to dress in pyjamas and get into bed. Then nurses and doctors came and talked to him, and all sorts of peculiar things happened like having his temperature taken, and being dressed in a kind of sheet tied with strings at the back. (*Bewildered, confused, puzzled.*) There was a boy in the next bed called Jake who was waiting to have his tonsils out too. After what seemed an age, a doctor came and said those fateful words, 'Just a little prick in your arm.'

The next thing Dan knew, he was lying on a trolley, and could see Mum's face looking rather fuzzy. He was in a strange room, and there were two nurses dressed in green and white clothes like sacks, with their hair in sort of green bags. 'What's hgoing on?' Dan said. His voice sounded rather far away, and his lips were dry.' (*Puzzled, confused.*) 'It's all done,' Mum said, grinning, 'Your tonsils are out and sitting in a jar.' (*Surprised, amazed, astonished.*)

By the next morning, Dan felt as fit as a flea, except for a slightly sore throat. Every meal seemed to include his favourite things, like jelly and ice-cream. There were several boys of his own age to muck about with in the day room. Dan really began to enjoy himself (*happy, cheerful*) and was quite disappointed when he was told he could go home, and Mum was coming to fetch him at three o'clock.

Stage III

Drawing Inference

Goody Goody!

1 Mum said, 'How lovely! Now we won't have to use the watering can.' (hosepipe)

2 Jo said, 'Yippee! Now I won't have to walk to school every morning.' (bike)

3 Dad said, 'This will mean puddles on the carpet I expect.' (puppy)

4 Jim said, 'This arrived just in time! I don't think the motor in the old one would have lasted much longer.' (car)

5 Mum said, 'I expect all the chairs will get scratched to bits, don't you?' (kitten)

6 Dad said, 'Great! This is one I've been wanting to read for ages.' (book)

7 Dad said, 'Put them on for me, let's see if they fit.' (slippers)

8 Sue said, 'I can't wait to have a bath, I'll put lots and lots of it in.' (bubble bath)

9 Mum said, 'Oh dear, fattening, but how delicious!' (chocolate)

10 Sam said, 'I'll let it go.' (balloon)

Goody Goody! (continued)

Stage III·

Drawing
Inference

Stage III

Drawing Inference

Travel Agent

Emma Smith is a nurse at the hospital. She works very hard at her job, and she looks forward to going on holiday with her friends. She loves the sun, swimming and water sports, but she hates doing her own cooking.

(Package holiday in hotel by sea, with available water sports.)

Mr and Mrs Brown have two children, Laura and Ben. They all like cycling and they often go for long bike rides together at the weekends. Mrs Brown collects china windmills.

(Cycling holiday in Holland, where it's very flat.)

John Hobbs works in a hotel. The busiest time is in the summer, so John takes his holidays in the winter. He doesn't like hot countries very much, and he's been having lessons at the dry ski slope.

(Skiing holiday.)

Katie Carter is a Science teacher. Her hobby is bird-watching. She is going on holiday with her friend this year, and they hope to see lots of new kinds of birds.

(Bird-watching holiday.)

Mr Jones is 75 years old, and he can't walk very well since he broke his leg. He loves boats.

(Cruise.)

There are five children in the *Baker* family. They haven't got enough money to go abroad for their holiday, and they all love being outdoors.

(Camping.)

Dave has just finished school. He's been saving his money for the big trip. He can't wait to set off on his adventure.

(Round-the-world ticket – India, Thailand, etc.)

Sue and Tim's daughter has gone to live in Australia with her husband.

(Australia.)

Puppet in the Playground

Incomplete Sentences

'…I think Sam pushed him over.' (crying child)

'…lucky the pond wasn't very deep.' (child dripping wet)

'…got caught up a tree.' (child holding kite)

'…wears her big sister's things.' (child in overlong skirt and jumper)

'…his birthday yesterday.' (child holding large toy car)

'…always brings some for Miss Manson at the beginning of term.' (girl holding bunch of flowers)

'…wants to take the whole class together.' (boy holding camera)

'…seems to feel the cold.' (child wearing gloves)

'…never eats his dinner.' (boy eating huge bun)

'…reckons she can keep it up for two whole minutes.' (girl skipping)

Stage IV

Drawing
Inference

Puppet in the Playground *(continued)*

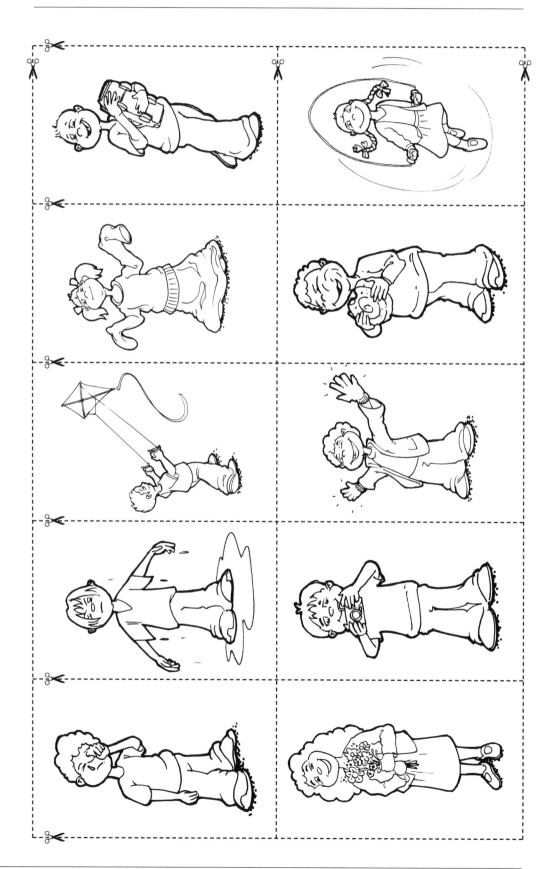

I Wonder

Stage IV

Drawing
Inference

Situations

Johnny is in the cupboard under the stairs.

Susie is running at top speed down the road.

David is fetching his torch.

Jane is standing beside a horse, with one hand on his neck.

Tom is creeping down the stairs in the middle of the night.

Jim is taking all the money out of his money box.

Dan is getting his Dad's ladder out of the garage.

Jo is climbing up a tree in her garden.

Debbie is getting some paper and a pencil out of a drawer.

Katie is peeping out of the window from behind the curtain.

Laura is putting lots of clothes into a suitcase.

Abbie is under the duvet, with her eyes shut.

Stage IV

Drawing Inference

Sixty-Second Stories

1 It was time to get up, but Sam snuggled down in bed and shut his eyes again. As usual, Mum had to come upstairs and pull the duvet off him. 'You're going to be late for school again, Sam,' she said. 'Haven't you been in enough trouble already?' (Question: 'Do you think Sam has ever been late for school?' Answer: 'Yes'.)

2 Jane was on her way to school, and was walking past the big field. There were usually cows in it, but today the cows were gone, and to Jane's surprise there was just a tiny, shaggy pony, about the size of a big dog. Jane wished she had some apple or a carrot in her pocket so she could feed him. (Question: 'Had Jane ever seen that pony before?' Answer: 'No'.)

3 Tim opened his lunch box. There was a Marmite sandwich, a Twix bar, a jam sandwich, and some sultanas. As she always did, Mum had included an apple, even though she knew perfectly well that Tim never ate it ... Mum never gave up. (Question: 'Was there an apple in the lunchbox?' Answer: 'Yes'.)

4 Anna burst in through the door, chucked her coat and school bag on the nearest chair, and ran into the kitchen where Mum was loading the washing machine. 'Mum, it's nice out, and I haven't got much homework to do. Can I go to Emma's house to play?' Mum looked up, surprised. 'But you never want to go to Emma's,' she said' 'What's changed all of a sudden?' (Question: 'Has Anna been to play at Emma's house before?' Answer: 'No'.)

5 Saturday morning! Gary looked out of the window. Today was the day for a second try at giving a barbecue. But it was raining – again! 'I think it always rains on Saturdays,' thought Gary. 'The summer will be over before we manage it.' But Dad had a good idea. 'We'll have it in the garage,' he said, 'with the doors open. Would that be OK?' (Question: 'Had they tried to give a barbecue before?' Answer: 'Yes'.)

6 Samantha opened the parcel from Grandma. As usual, it was a strange knitted object, which looked as if Grandma had been using up lots of different old balls of wool. Samantha held it up against herself and looked in the mirror. There seemed to be two sleeves, and a hole for the head to go through, so she supposed it was a jumper. It was always difficult to know what to say to Grandma, who meant to be so kind. (Question: 'Had Grandma knitted something for Samantha before?' Answer: 'Yes'.)

Find Fred

Stage IV

Drawing
Inference

1 Fred sat by the window, staring out. It took some time for his eyes to get used to the dark outside. Suddenly Fred nearly jumped out of his skin. Just ouside the window was a huge fish, looking in at HIM! As Fred looked more closely, he could see other smaller fish swimming about between the rocks and around the broken mast of the old ship. Then the engine noise got louder, and they zoomed away to find another wreck.

2 Fred peered out. The sun was just coming up. In the distance, Fred could see mountains, while far below him he could see fields and houses, looking tiny, like ones in a toy farm set. Then suddenly he couldn't see anything, and realised that they were in a cloud. As they passed through the cloud, he could first see a bit of the wing, then one of the engines and the tip of the wing, and finally they were out again, and clouds were floating by underneath them.

3 Fred sat in his corner seat, where he could keep an eye on the corridor, and look out of the window at the same time. The engine gathered speed, and they were soon out of the town and rushing through the countryside. They passed fields full of cows and sheep, then some woods. Then they were beside a road, and racing the cars. Some children were standing on a bridge over the road. They waved and Fred waved back, but they probably couldn't see him. The wheels went clackety-clack, clackety-clack, and then they began to slow down for the next station.

Stage IV

Drawing
Inference

Find Fred *(continued)*

4 Fred stood just inside the big double doors. There seemed to be hundreds of children about. There was a row of pegs just inside the door, with names written above them, and lots of coats hanging up. Some of the pegs had bags on as well. More and more children kept coming through the doors, some with grownups, who kissed them goodbye, and went away again. Fred was beginning to wonder what he was supposed to do, and to feel a bit tearful, when a grown up came and took his hand. 'You must be Fred,' she said kindly. 'Come this way and I'll show you your classroom!'

5 Fred looked around. There was a funny smell, and it was very warm. The big high-ceilinged building echoed with shouts and laughter. Every so often there would be a thud and a splash. Sometimes a whistle blew, and the instructor told somebody off for jumping in off the side. Fred could see one brave boy up on the topmost board, his arms up as he got ready for his dive. At the shallow end some small children were practising with armbands and rubber rings. Fred turned to go to the changing rooms and get into his swimming trunks.

6 Fred grabbed hold of the trolley and set off, steering carefully. In through the big revolving doors, past the stand with the newspapers and magazines on it, and the display Fred always liked, with huge buckets of flowers and potted plants. He weaved his way past the fruit and vegetables, stopping whenever Dad said 'Stop'. Dad was studying his list, and putting loads of things into the trolley. 'Deli counter now,' Dad said, 'And then we need the dairy section'. Fred hoped he might get some sweets at the checkout, as a thank you for pushing the trolley.

Monster Collection

Stage II

Describing

Suspect!

Speechmark Ⓟ This page may be photocopied for instructional use only. *Speaking, Listening & Understanding*
© C Delamain & J Spring 2003

Spiders' Webs

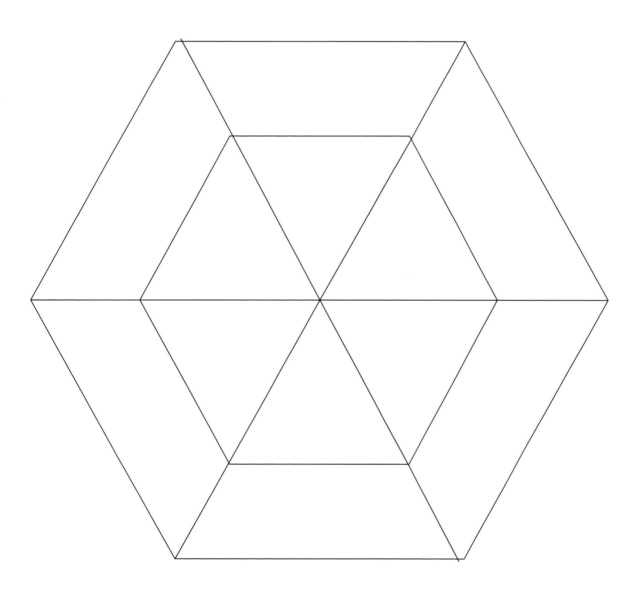

Stage I

Explaining

They Belong

Picture Grid

Enlarge the grid as necessary, then cut into individual pictures.

Stage I

Explaining

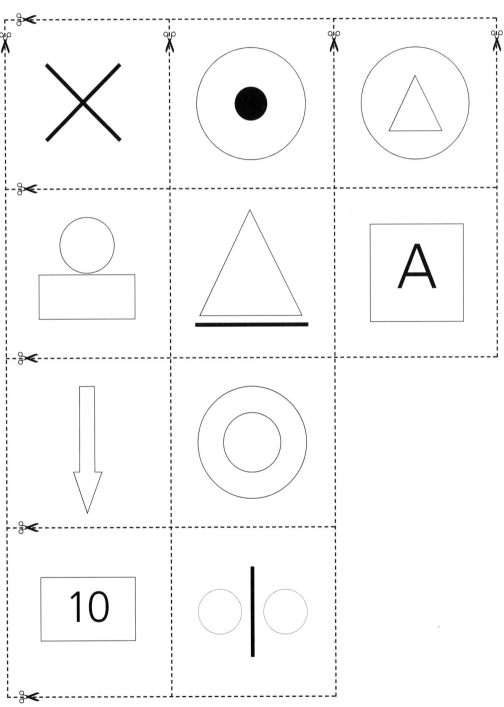

Stage II

Explaining

Match Mine

Speechmark **P** This page may be photocopied for instructional use only. *Speaking, Listening & Understanding*
© C Delamain & J Spring 2003

Claim It

Stage II

Explaining

Because

Child alone crying by a bus stop.

Child standing fully clothed on the edge of a swimming pool.

Man running down the road after another man.

Woman smiling and waving her arms in the air.

Man approaching house carrying a ladder.

Very young child picking up the telephone.

Car parked by the side of the road with the driver leaning against the bonnet.

Workmen erecting a barrier at the entrance to a road.

Tracks

Tracks *(continued)*

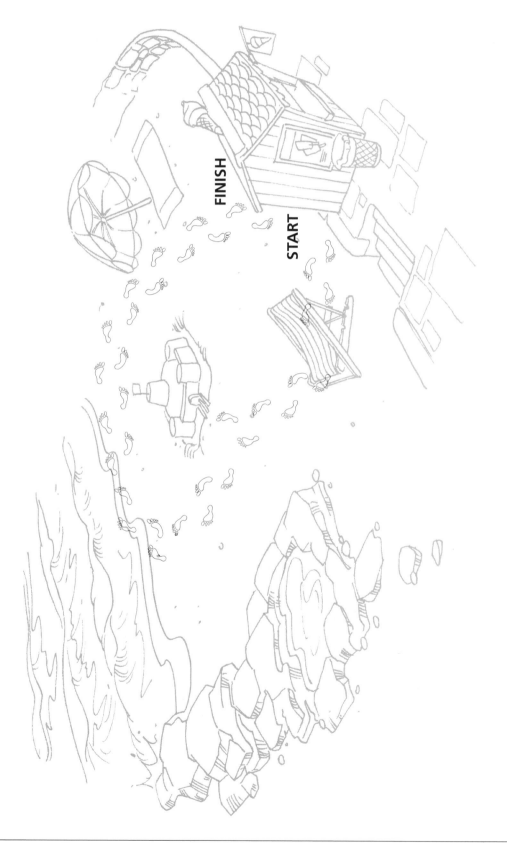

FINISH

START

Tracks (continued)

Stage IV

Explaining

Stage IV

Explaining

Tracks *(continued)*

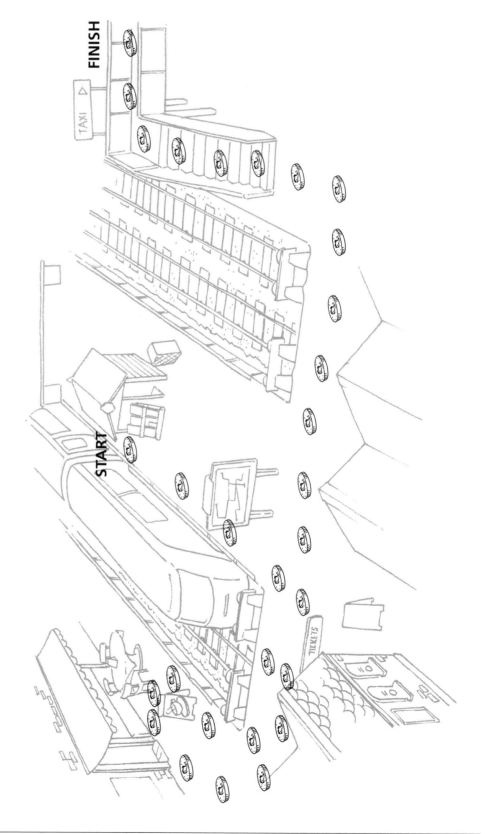

Speechmark Ⓟ This page may be photocopied for instructional use only. *Speaking, Listening & Understanding*
© C Delamain & J Spring 2003

Tracks *(continued)*

Stage IV

Explaining

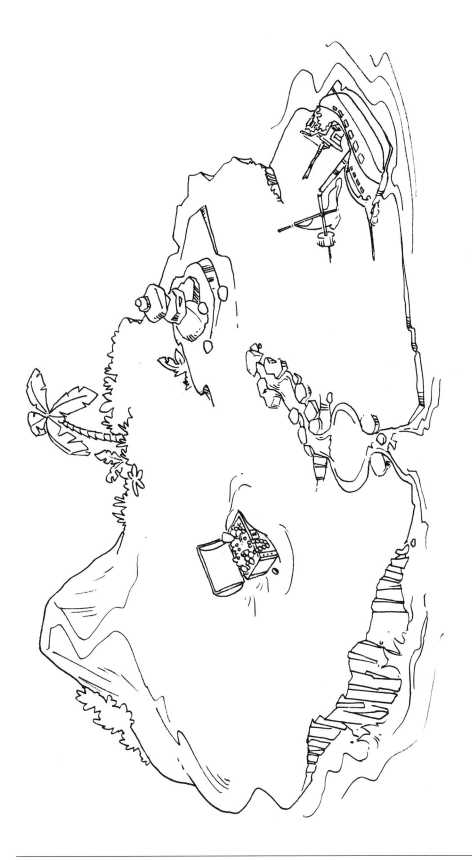

Stage IV

Explaining

Tracks *(continued)*

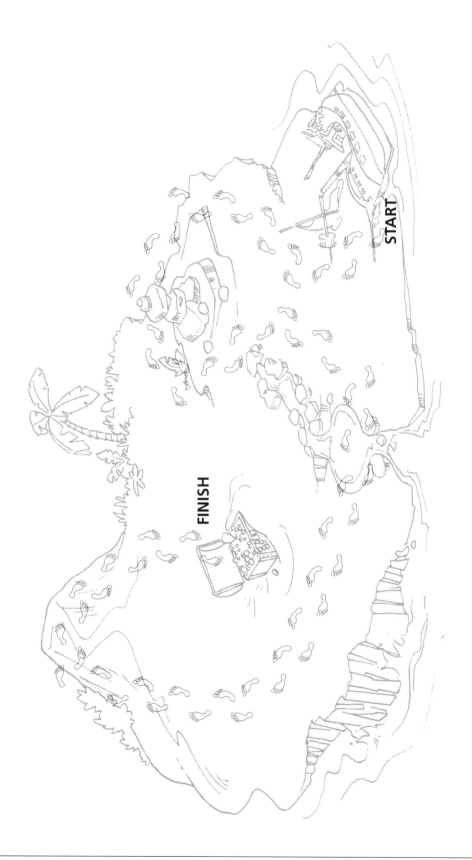

Speechmark (S) (P) This page may be photocopied for instructional use only. *Speaking, Listening & Understanding*
© C Delamain & J Spring 2003

Tracks *(continued)*

Stage IV

Explaining

Tracks *(continued)*

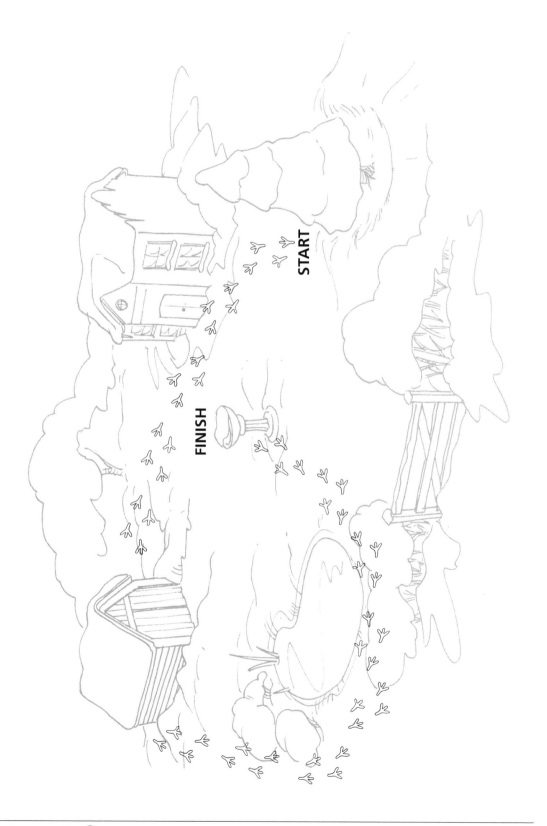

Speechmark Ⓟ This page may be photocopied for instructional use only. *Speaking, Listening & Understanding*
© C Delamain & J Spring 2003

Tracks *(continued)*

Stage IV

Explaining

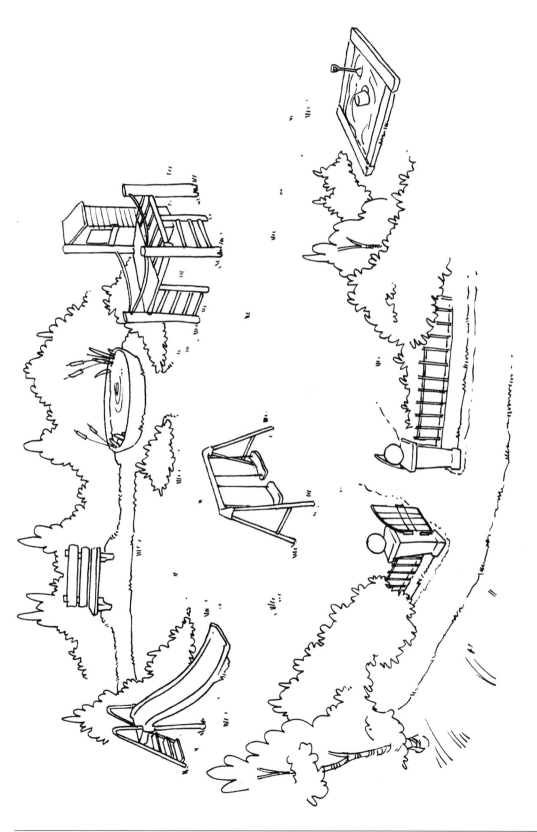

Stage IV

Explaining

Tracks *(continued)*

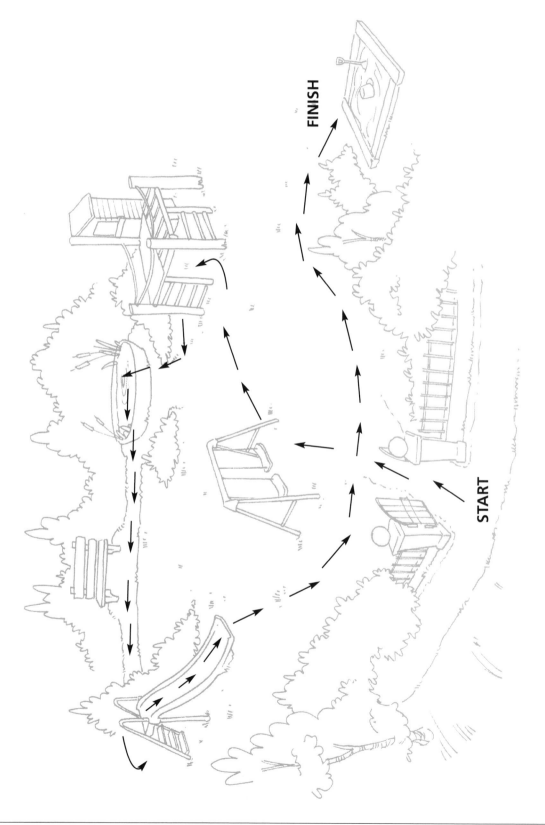

Second Half

Stage II

Narrating

'When I was a baby I…'

'I do like chocolate, but…'

'If we could fly we…'

'Fish can't walk because…'

'I sometimes fall asleep while…'

'I'll have to wait for new shoes until…'

'I go to watch the match whenever…'

'I shan't be going out whatever…'

Then you can turn some of them round the other way:

'I didn't like it when…'

'We would be happy if…'

'Because he was late …'

'While she was riding her bike…'

'Until you are older…'

'Whenever we go on the bus…'

'Whatever Mum says…'

At a later stage, you could include a variation on this activity in the Literacy Hour. Give the children one of the incomplete sentences, without the key word. Offer a choice of the key words. The children can select an appropriate one, and complete the sentence using it.

Stage IV

Narrating

Hatch-a-Plot

Prediction Pairs

If you don't brush your teeth	they will go rotten.
Mix blue and yellow	and make green.
When it snows	you need warm clothes.
If you stroke a cat	it will probably purr.
If you run very fast	you will get puffed out.
Mix blue and red	and make purple.
If you throw a stone at a window	the glass will smash.
If you go to bed late	you will be tired in the morning.
Leave chocolate in the sun	and it will melt.
If you keep a pet	you must take care of it.
If you plant some seeds	they will grown into plants.
When it rains	you need an umbrella.
Children need fruit	to keep them healthy.
You must keep ice-cream	in the freezer.
A bird makes a nest	to lay eggs in.

Predicting

Look Out!

Examples:

A little boy is leaning out over the fence to look at the sea lions.

A lady with pretend fruit on her hat is walking past the giraffe enclosure.

A man is gardening, and he has put his sandwiches on the bird-table.

Two birds are pulling at opposite ends of a worm.

A girl is pushing a shopping trolley down a steep slope to the car-park.

A very big man is about to sit down on a chair where the cat is asleep.

A boy is walking under the painter's ladder.

A lorry is backing towards the edge of a cliff.

A cat has its paw in the top of the fish tank.

Challenge the children to come up with two alternative predictions.

Poor Mr Pig

Stage II

Predicting

(Story One, Version One)

When you try this first story, read it *slowly*, and emphasise the points at which you hope the children will spot disaster potential. These points are in italics. Probable predictions are in parentheses. When you progress to the second story, you can try speeding up and not giving any clues.

Mr Pig looked out of his window and saw that it was a lovely sunny day. He badly wanted to go to the beach, but his car was being mended. 'Never mind,' he thought, 'I'll take Mrs Pig's little minicar, she won't need it today.' He packed a big picnic basket, and *climbed into the car* (got stuck.) Off down the road he went. When he reached the seaside, he popped into a shop to buy a sun-hat and a lilo. He went in *through the revolving doors* (got stuck again), and up in the *lift, which was very small.* (Stuck once more.) When he had finished his shopping, he waddled down to the beach, and lowered himself *into a deckchair.* (Chair broke.) He took out his packet of sandwiches and had just one. After a bit he got quite hot, so he unpacked his swimming trunks. He hadn't worn them for a long time, so he was a bit worried they wouldn't fit. He wrapped himself in a towel, undressed, and *pulled on his trunks.* (Trunks split.) Then he blew up his lilo, and went down to the water. He launched the lilo on to the little waves, and *lay down on it.* (Lilo sank.) Mr Pig floated peacefully, dabbling his trotters in the water. After a while, he began to feel hungry, something that happened to him very often. He came out of the sea, and went back to where he had left his things. A quick rub dry, and *down sat Mr Pig* all ready for his picnic. (Sat on sandwiches and squashed them.) After lunch and a little nap, Mr Pig packed up and went off to where there were some little wooden steps leading up to the road. *Up the steps he went* (steps broke), found his car, and drove happily home. (8 POINTS)

Poor Mr Pig (Story One, Version Two)

Mr Pig looked out of his window and saw that it was a lovely sunny day. He badly wanted to go to the beach, but his car was being mended. 'Never mind,' he thought, 'I'll take Mrs Pig's little minicar, she won't need it today.' He packed a big picnic basket, and climbed into the car. He could hardly fit behind the steering wheel, and couldn't move his fat little legs to press the pedals at all. 'This won't do', he thought, and tried to get out, but he was stuck fast. He had to call to several passers-by, and there was a lot of pulling and pushing and grunting (and it wasn't only Mr Pig who was grunting) before he finally shot out of the car like a cork out of a bottle. Mr Pig took the bus instead, and off he went to the seaside. He popped into a shop to buy a sun-hat and a lilo. He

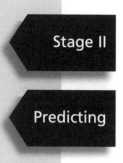

Stage II

Predicting

Poor Mr Pig *(continued)*

went in through the revolving doors, just managing to fit into one of the sections. Round went the door, and Mr Pig tried to go out the other side, but he was wedged fast. Round and round he went in the revolving door until he was getting quite giddy. At last one of the shop assistants saw what was happening. When she had finished laughing, she had the door stopped and two strong men heaved Mr Pig out. You will hardly believe this, but the same thing happened when he went up in the lift! Luckily, this time there was somebody standing behind him who could push, and push he did until Mr Pig almost fell out. When he had finished his shopping, he decided it would be safer to leave by the stairs and a side door.

At the beach, Mr Pig waddled down the sand and lowered himself into a deckchair. There was a terrible cracking and splitting sound as the chair collapsed, and Mr Pig hit the sand with a bump. The deckchair attendant was not pleased, and warned that he would have to charge Mr Pig for the cost of a chair. Mr Pig settled for sitting on his rug. After a bit he got quite hot, and decided to go for a swim. Wrapping himself in his towel, he undressed and struggled to get into his old swimming trunks. He heaved and tugged, and they were nearly up when with a tearing sound they ripped from top to bottom. Mr Pig was at a loss what to do, but a kind lady sitting nearby said it would be quite all right to swim in his shorts.

Mr Pig blew up his Lilo, and launched it on the little waves. With a happy shout he flopped down on to it. Immediately the Lilo tipped and sank, and Mr Pig got several mouthfuls of salt water before he got on to his trotters again.

After his swim, Mr Pig felt hungry. A quick rub dry, and down sat Mr Pig all ready for his picnic. He looked round for his sandwiches. He knew he had taken them out of the picnic basket. Where could they be? He stood up again, and wondered why a little boy nearby was laughing and pointing at him. He felt round behind himself. There was something damp and squishy there, stuck on his shorts. His sandwiches! Poor Mr Pig had to make do with an ice-cream from an ice-cream stall along the beach. It was time to go home. Mr Pig gathered up his possessions, and made for the wooden steps leading up to the road. But there was one more disaster to come. The steps creaked and groaned under Mr Pig's weight, and then collapsed. Mr Pig had to walk a long way along the beach before he found some nice strong concrete steps to go up instead.

When he got home, Mrs Pig met him at the door. 'Don't ask if I've had a lovely day,' said Mr Pig, 'Just don't ask!'

Poor Mr Pig *(continued)*

Story Two, Version One

If the children have heard the first Mr Pig story, read this one at normal speed, and don't emphasise the points that they children are supposed to spot. You might try seating the children facing outwards away from each other, so they cannot copy.

Mr Pig looked out of his window, and saw that it was beginning to snow. Mr Pig just loved snow, and that day it snowed and snowed until the drifts came almost up to the kitchen windowsill. When it stopped and the sun came out, Mr Pig put on his snow-suit, boots, and woolly hat, and went out into the garden. Mr Pig started gingerly *down the icy garden path* (slipped over) and into the garage. He knew he had an old sledge somewhere. Yes, there it was, slung up on the ceiling. Mr Pig took hold of the rope that was holding it up, and began to *lower the sledge.* (Comes down and hits him on the head.) He dusted it off, and carried it up the little hill beside his house. Carefully, he sat down on the sledge, pushed off with his trotters, and set off with a whoosh! down the hill. At the bottom of the hill the snow had piled up *into a huge drift.* (Sledge ploughs into drift.) Mr Pig played with his sledge for ages, and several children came out to join him. Then they went to the nearby duck pond to see if it was frozen. It was! Mr Pig said he would be first on to the ice, to check that it was safe. *One step on the ice, two steps.* (He goes through the ice.) 'It's OK boys and girls,' he shouted. They had a wonderful time sliding about on the ice, and a game of ice hockey using sticks and a stone. The next thing, of course, was a snowball fight. They went back to Mr Pig's garden, and formed into two teams. Mr Pig got a snowball right on his snout. He was determined to hit the boy who had thrown it. The boy was standing near the kitchen window. Mr Pig took careful aim, and *threw the snowball with all his might.* (Hits kitchen window and breaks it.) 'Gottim!' he yelled. 'We're coming to get you!' shouted the boys, and they began to chase Mr Pig. Mr Pig ran out of the garden and set off across the fields. The snow got deeper and deeper, and Mr Pig's *trotters began to sink deeper and deeper too.* (Sinks into snow and gets stuck.) But he managed to keep going. After a bit, the children got tired of the game, and Mr Pig made his weary way home to the fire and a cup of tea. (6 POINTS)

Story Two, Version Two

Mr Pig looked out of his window, and saw that it was beginning to snow. Mr Pig just loved snow, and that day it snowed and snowed until the drifts came almost up to the kitchen windowsill. When it stopped and the sun came out, Mr Pig put on his snow-suit, boots, and woolly hat, and went out into the

Stage II

Predicting

Poor Mr Pig *(continued)*

garden. Mr Pig was starting gingerly down the icy garden path when whoops! his trotters went from under him, and he sat down hard on the path, bending his curly tail underneath him. He got up, and going even more carefully made his way to the garage. He knew he had an old sledge somewhere. Yes, there it was, slung up on the ceiling. Mr Pig took hold of the rope that was holding it up, and began to lower the sledge. All at once, the rope slipped through his trotters, and the sledge came down on his head with a thump. Poor Mr Pig rubbed his head. His eyes were smarting. When he felt a bit better, he dusted the sledge down, and carried it up the little hill beside his house. Carefully, he sat down on the sledge, pushed off with his trotters, and set off with a whoosh! down the hill. At the bottom of the hill the snow had piled up into a huge drift. With Mr Pig's weight on board, there was no stopping the sledge, and it slammed into the drift at 20 miles an hour. Snow flew everywhere. Mr Pig brushed the snow out of his eyes and ears, and emptied the snow from his boots. Some children came out to play too, and after a bit they went to the duck pond to see if it was frozen. It was! Mr Pig said he would be first on to the ice, to check that it was safe. One step on the ice, two steps…a resounding crack, and Mr Pig found himself standing up to his hocks in freezing water. 'It's not safe boys and girls,' said Mr Pig, 'Let's have a snowball fight instead.' Back in Mr Pig's garden, they formed into two teams. Mr Pig got a snowball right on his snout. He was determined to hit the boy who had thrown it. The boy was standing near the kitchen window. Mr Pig took careful aim, and threw the snowball with all his might. The boy ducked, the snowball sailed on, and straight through the kitchen window, with a splintering of glass. The children began to run away. Mr Pig set off after them, but the snow got deeper and deeper, and Mr Pig sank deeper and deeper too. At last he gave up, and floundering and gasping he reached the road. He made his way home, cold, wet and weary. When Mrs Pig came back, Mr Pig opened the door to her. 'Don't ask if I've had fun in the snow!,' he said, 'Just don't ask!'

What Can We Do?

1 Bob is going to be late for the football match.

2 Zoe has just come out of the hairdresser's with a trendy new haircut.

3 Sam is opening his birthday present – a new bike, which he didn't think he'd get.

4 Rashid has eaten too many chocolates and is feeling sick.

5 Emma has just woken up in the night, and she can hear something banging against the window.

6 Mum has just walked into the kitchen to find the whole floor flooded.

7 Beth has just walked into the playground of her new school.

8 Charlene has accidentally just broken her mum's best vase.

9 Gary has been stung by a bee.

10 Sophie has just found out that the school trip to the beach has been cancelled.

11 Jack has won the football trophy, and is walking up to the stage to receive it.

12 Ben's hamster has died.

Stage IV

Predicting

Raffle Prize

1 Errol and his dad love football. His dad plays in the local team and they both support Liverpool.

2 Nassim is the artist in the class. He is longing for a proper set of watercolour paints, and has been saving up for ages.

3 Emily's favourite colour is pink, and guess why? Yes, she loves Barbie and she's got six different Barbie® dolls. She likes swapping Barbie clothes with her friends.

4 Zak is nearly seven. He's got a grown-up stepbrother who plays the guitar in a band. Zak thinks his stepbrother is really cool, and he hopes when he's older he can join the band too.

5 Laura wants to be a vet when she grows up. She just loves animals, and she's got a cat and two hamsters.

6 Sophie had her ears pierced last weekend. It felt a bit funny at the time, but now she's really pleased because it makes her feel grown up.

7 Rachel is very sporty. She likes riding, cycling and swimming. She's just learnt to swim under water, and finds she can go much faster.

8 Errol loves watching motor racing on TV, but nobody else in the house likes it, and somebody always turns it off when the race is halfway through.

THE PRIZES
1 A football.
2 Some money.
3 A pram.
4 A drum kit.
5 A goldfish.
6 A pair of earrings.
7 Swimming goggles.
8 A television.

Raffle Prize *(continued)*

Stage II

Playing
With Words

Ridiculous Rhymes

There once was a very cool cat
Who liked to go out in a... (hat)

A man saw a very large mouse
He said 'Get that out of my...' (house)

A boy had caught such a big fish
Mum said, 'It won't fit on the...' (dish)

'Nice biscuits,' said Jack, 'I'll have four'
 Mum said 'You can't have any...' (more)

Said Mary, 'I've got a new pen'
Said Tommy, 'So what, I've got...' (ten)

Poor Billy got wet in a puddle
Kind grandmother gave him a... (cuddle)

Said Johnny, 'You know what I'd like
A beautiful two-wheeler...' (bike)

There was only one more piece of toast
And Dad had already had... (most)

Freddie the very small frog
Said, 'Oh dear, now I'm lost in the...' (fog)

'There's a picture of you in this book'
Said Dad, 'come on over and...' (look)

Word Stew

dog	crisps	house	17
rabbit	burger	church	24
cat	pizza	hospital	125
horse	ice-cream	school	2
elephant	chips	shop	89
lion	sausages	bungalow	47
pig	apple	castle	540
fox	banana	lighthouse	9
bed	football	Spain	shirt
chair	tennis	England	dress
table	hockey	France	tracksuit
cupboard	basketball	America	socks
bookcase	skating	Germany	sweatshirt
stool	netball	India	jumper
wardrobe	swimming	Italy	jeans
sofa	rugby	Africa	pyjamas
desk	judo	China	coat

UNDERSTANDING SPOKEN LANGUAGE: RECORD SHEET

Key: needs adult support ◹ almost achieved ⊠ achieved ▦

Child's Name	Following Instructions				Developing Vocabulary				Getting the Main Idea				Thinking Skills				Drawing Inference			
	I	II	III	IV	I	II	III	IV	I	II	III	IV	I	II	III	IV	I	II	III	IV

Speechmark

℗ This page may be photocopied for instructional use only. *Speaking, Listening & Understanding*
© C Delamain & J Spring 2003

USING SPOKEN LANGUAGE: RECORD SHEET

Key: needs adult support ◻ almost achieved ⬔ achieved ⬛

Child's Name	Describing I	II	III	IV	Explaining I	II	III	IV	Narrating I	II	III	IV	Predicting I	II	III	IV	Playing with Words I	II	III	IV

Bibliography

Ackroyd J, 2000, *Literacy Alive!,* Hodder & Stoughton, London.

Berger & Gross, *Teaching the Literacy Hour in an Inclusive Classroom,* David Fulton Publications, London.

Booth D, *Reading the Stories we Construct Together,* Literacy Alive! Hodder & Stoughton, London.

Booth D, 1998, *Guiding the Reading Process*, Pembroke Publishers.

Delamain C & Spring J, 2000, *Developing Baseline Communication Skills,* Speechmark Publishing Ltd, Bicester.

Lock A, Ginsborg J & Peers I, 2002, 'Development and Disadvantage: Implications for the Early Years and Beyond', *International Journal of Language and Communication Disorders,* 37 (1).

Ripley K, Barrett J & Fleming P, 2001, *Inclusion for Children with Speech and Language Impairment,* David Fulton Publishers, London.

Sage R, 2000, *The Communication Opportunity Group Scheme*, Leicester University Press, Leicester.